HEAVEN'S TOUCH

A story about Trials, Love, and Faith.

GABBY CORNELIO

Cover by Gabby Cornelio
Illustrations by Gabby Cornelio
First printed edition 2025

The Cokeville Miracle (film, 2015). Directed by T.C. Christensen. Based on true events that occurred in 1986 in Cokeville, Wyoming. This book references the film The Cokeville Miracle as an example of faith and divine protection in extreme circumstances. All rights belong to its creators.

Musical references:
Daigle, L. (2023). Thank God I Do. On Lauren Daigle [album]. Atlantic Records.
Day, N. (2020). I Will Go and Do. On Come Unto Christ: 2020 Youth Album [Album].

HEAVEN'S TOUCH

A story about Trials, Love, and Faith.

GABBY CORNELIO

ACKNOWLEDGMENTS

I want to thank my husband, Jorge. Who has been a strong and constant support. Thanks to his hard work, I have been able to dedicate the necessary time to care for our three children. Jorge has inspired me to pursue my dreams, always pushing and motivating me when I feel discouraged. I am grateful for him being my partner and confidant, making our journey together both beautiful and joyful.

To my children, Abby, Mahonri, and Moroni, because through motherhood, I have become a better version of myself.

To my mother-in-law, Mama Carmen, who has been an incredible help in these past months, allowing me the time to write this book.

I also want to express my gratitude to the two most courageous women I know—my mom, Vivi, and my grandmother, Carmita. Their example has been a great inspiration in my life.

CONTENIDO

INTRODUCTION

Hello, my name is Gabby Cornelio, and I am excited to share my life story with you.

I was born into a family that has lived by religious principles. My mother and grandmother taught me to love God and Jesus Christ and to put them first in my life, praying daily for guidance and protection. For me, it was easy to love them because I enjoyed reading the Scriptures, attending church—where I was spiritually nourished—and serving others.

Because I was so happy in my childhood and youth while following the teachings of Jesus Christ, I longed to share that happiness with others. At the age of 21, I decided to serve an eighteen-month religious mission, which meant leaving my parents, siblings, friends, and hometown behind. During that time, I dedicated myself to preaching the Gospel of Jesus Christ. Those eighteen months were a time of great spiritual growth, during which I developed skills and virtues I didn't have before. I gained a deeper understanding of the Scriptures, and strengthened my personal testimony of God, Jesus Christ, and the Holy Spirit.

I will always cherish that time, as I met many people from whom I learned great lessons and had missionary companions whom I came to love and accept just as they are.

Because of that service I gave to God, I have received countless blessings to this day. Everything I experienced during that time helped me make good decisions in my life. Among those decisions, one of the most important was choosing my husband, Jorge González. Our Heavenly Father gave us the greatest blessing—being parents to three beautiful children whom we love with all our hearts: Abby, Mahonri, and Moroni.

Our life has been a true adventure, like a roller coaster. We embarked on this journey expecting to experience fun, joy, and happiness. In my youth, I didn't know that the climbs would be so thrilling and rewarding, nor did I imagine that the descents would be so painful and dark. However, through this adventure, we have created a little piece of heaven here on earth.

I have learned through personal experience that the ups and downs of life are essential to our personal and family growth. Every turn, every stop, every climb, and every drop are necessary to enjoy this journey called life.

One of the descents in our roller coaster began when I struggled to conceive. From the moment we got married, Jorge and I dreamed of having children right away, but that didn't happen. Despite all our efforts, that long-awaited dream didn't come. I was sincerely happy when my relatives, friends, and acquaintances announced their pregnancies. However, at the same time, my heart broke because I couldn't carry a baby in my own womb.

In His mercy, God blessed us with Abby, who came into our lives after a few years. Two years after Abby's birth, we welcomed

Mahonri. The joy we felt as we climbed that mountain was indescribable. My love and trust in the Lord grew stronger every day through these blessings.

But soon, an unexpected turn came. We had always wanted a large family, so we continued praying and fasting, asking the Lord to bless us with more children. One day, to our surprise, I found out I was pregnant again! However, our happiness didn't last long because I miscarried in 2017, and then again in 2018.

The loss in 2018 was especially painful. I was about three months pregnant when I began experiencing intense abdominal pain, which led me to the hospital. It was there that I learned I was having a miscarriage. The pain was constant and excruciating.

A nurse approached me to administer morphine. The nurse didn't know I was allergic to it, and within seconds, my body reacted violently. My throat closed, my body began shaking uncontrollably, and I couldn't breathe or move. I felt myself losing control of my body and consciousness. In an instant, everything went dark.

At that moment—on the brink of death—I heard a voice telling me, **"Open your eyes, open your eyes."** I wanted to obey, but I couldn't; I had no strength. I felt like I was returning to my heavenly home. However, I made an immense effort to follow that voice.

I managed to open my eyes and saw doctors and nurses rushing around me, trying to stabilize me. I knew I was in a critical moment, and if I wanted to live, I had to turn to God.

In my mind, I began pleading with my Father:

"I am so grateful for the two children You have given me. They need me. If You let me live, I promise I will never ask You for more children again. From now on, I will be grateful

for the two You have already blessed me with, I will love them, and I will be the best mother to them."

It took several hours for my body to stabilize and stop shaking, but I survived the allergic reaction to morphine.

I kept my promise to the Lord. I stopped asking for more children and devoted myself entirely to Abby and Mahonri. Accepting that I wouldn't have more children brought peace to my life. I lived fully and with gratitude for the small family I had.

We had new plans, and our life was going well. But to my surprise, God had other plans for our family. Without asking for it, God sent us an angel.

It may sound strange, but I didn't pray for Moroni as I had for my other children. This doesn't mean I didn't long for him; I simply didn't ask for him because I had made a promise to God not to ask for more children, and I had kept that promise until that moment. However, in my heart, Moroni was just as deeply desired as my other children. God knew the feelings of my soul—the deep desire for another child—and He granted me that blessing.

I discovered the pregnancy in such an unexpected way. We were having dinner, one of my favorite meals that included broccoli, when suddenly, I ran to the bathroom feeling nauseous. My sister-in-law immediately said I was pregnant. To me, it was a joke. I assured her I wasn't, but she didn't hesitate and ran to buy me a pregnancy test. To my surprise, it was positive!

This pregnancy was different; I experienced abdominal pain almost constantly. At every check-up, doctors simply told me to drink water and take pain medication. It was tough. I was deeply saddened because I felt that something was wrong, but my own doctor ignored me.

One afternoon, at 33 weeks pregnant, I felt an urgent need to go to the emergency room due to severe pain and contractions. The doctor on duty contacted my OB-GYN, and they both agreed it was nothing serious and sent me home. I returned home discouraged, but I knew something was happening with either me or my baby.

Two weeks later, Moroni was born.

From the moment he arrived, our lives changed drastically. From a very young age, he had to undergo multiple surgeries and endure immense physical suffering. In the midst of these challenges and the darkest moments, I learned something I never would have discovered had we not gone through these trials with our son Moroni.

I chose the title of my book because, in the deepest darkness, I felt heavenly arms embracing me, tender hands touching me. I felt the presence of God, my Redeemer Jesus Christ, the Holy Spirit, and angels ministering to me.

Through all the challenges we have faced, I have developed a deep closeness with my Heavenly Father. This unique bond with Him has been forged through the refining fire of each experience.

I have written my story to share both the physical and spiritual experiences we have lived, the emotions that emerged, and the life lessons learned.

I know I'm not the only person in the world who has gone through difficult times. At some point in our lives, we will all face different kinds of problems, challenges, afflictions, and trials— because we are on this earth with a purpose. This book will help you discover yours. But life is not all about suffering. Our

Heavenly Father wants us to experience joy, happiness, peace, and, above all, to learn how to live by faith. And even though life may sometimes feel overwhelming, I can testify that with God's guiding hand, everything becomes easier. We can all access the light of Christ—a light that shines in the midst of darkness.

This book is meant to help you know and draw closer to the most special Beings who exist—those who can lift and sustain you: God, my Heavenly Father, whom I love deeply, and His Son Jesus Christ, my Savior, my light, my guide, and my hope.

Some time ago, I heard a leader from the church I attend, The Church of Jesus Christ of Latter-day Saints, speak at a conference. Elder Dieter F. Uchtdorf encouraged us to "share what is in our hearts." I've reflected often on those words and realized that there are so many things in my heart I want to share with the world.

That reflection inspired me to write this book. My intention is to reach your heart and fill it with love, hope, and faith.

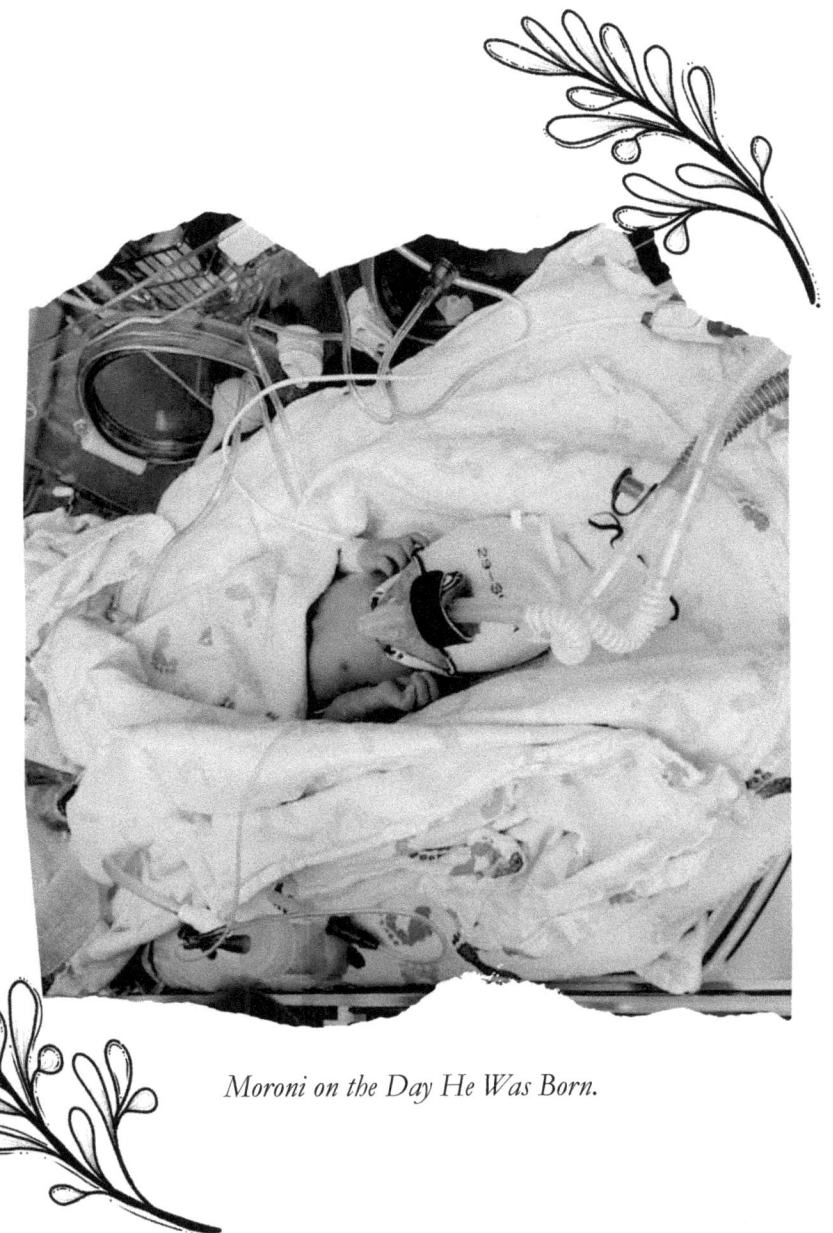

Moroni on the Day He Was Born.

CHAPTER 1

A PRAYER FROM THE HEART

"Then you will call upon Me and come
and pray to Me, and I will listen to you.
You will seek Me and find Me when you
seek Me with all your heart."

- Jeremiah 29:12–13

I was 33 weeks pregnant. I went to my OB-GYN's office without an appointment because I wasn't feeling well. The clinic refused to see me and told me to go to the emergency room, so I did.

But the doctor on duty once again said everything was fine, without even performing an ultrasound. He just looked at me and said it was normal to feel pain.

I got home and went straight to bed; I felt very distressed, with a deep sense of knowing that something was wrong. Then I remembered I had the private phone number of a gynecologist I'd known years ago. I decided to call him, and when we spoke, he told me I shouldn't be feeling that way. He said he could see me that same afternoon and do an ultrasound.

He was incredibly kind to make time for me, even though he didn't really know me anymore, it had been so long. When I arrived, he did the ultrasound right away. As he scanned, he was very serious and didn't say a single word. Once he finished, he simply said I needed to see a specialist at another hospital the following week.

That appointment happened to fall on our wedding anniversary. We were celebrating nine years of marriage and were happy, thinking we would confirm that everything was fine.

They performed a very detailed ultrasound where we could see the baby's heart, stomach, and many other parts. Red and blue images showed up on the screen. The doctor remained silent, and I couldn't tell if things were good or bad.

When he finished, he told us I had polyhydramnios—an excessive buildup of amniotic fluid, which occurs in only 1% to 2% of pregnancies. The cause, he explained, was a likely genetic condition in the baby.

He said Moroni had a heart problem and possibly Down Syndrome. Although we had done early genetic testing that had come back negative, he didn't understand how those results could've been wrong.

He also told us Moroni's intestines were not connected and that he had duodenal atresia, which would require surgery right after birth. He warned us that if I had to go to the ER at any point, I couldn't go just anywhere—only two hospitals in Dallas and the surrounding area had the proper equipment to handle Moroni's case.

It was a devastating day for us as a couple. We had no idea what the future held. I was physically miserable, barely able to walk, and afraid my baby might not survive.

It was a moment of deep sorrow, but I didn't have time to process it—Moroni was born just one week later due to persistent contractions and the risk of my uterus rupturing. I had previously had surgery to remove a uterine tumor, along with two C-sections from my older children.

I pleaded with the doctor to let me wait one more week. I told him I could bear the pain, since Moroni was still so small. I thought if I could just hold on, he might grow more. But the doctor refused, saying both our lives were at risk.

The day Moroni was born was filled with fear. Right after birth, he was rushed away due to breathing problems and heart complications, so I didn't get to meet him that day—it wasn't until the next.

Moroni was tiny, weighing just 4 pounds, and he had his first surgery at two days old to connect his intestines. During recovery, he spent two weeks with tubes in his mouth and nose, receiving nutrition intravenously.

We prayed and begged for him to poop—this would be a sign that his intestines were working.

That experience made me reflect on how grateful we should be for the basic functions of the body—things we so often take for granted.

Moroni's face looked different. He didn't resemble my other children. His eyes bulged, the folds of his eyelids were wide, and his tongue was almost always out.

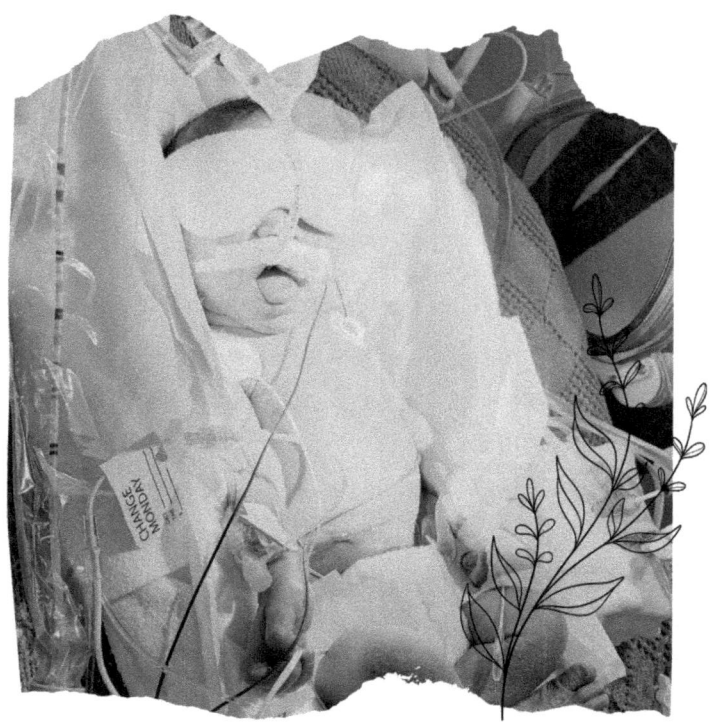

At first, I thought it was because of the tube in his mouth. I kept asking the doctor why he looked like that. They ran genetic tests to check for Down Syndrome, but the results came back negative. The doctors said he was swollen and just needed time.

God answered our prayers—Moroni was able to eat and have a bowel movement. It was a moment of tremendous joy, a sign that he was healing. They also told us his heart looked okay. Eventually, Moroni was discharged from the hospital. It was one of our first joyful moments—finally bringing our baby home so his siblings could meet him.

Due to the COVID-19 pandemic, they hadn't been allowed in the hospital. Despite everything, the joy of that moment—when they first met their baby brother—was priceless.

The first months of Moroni's life were incredibly difficult. Every time I tried to feed him, I faced situations I didn't understand. He had trouble latching onto the bottle, and when he did, something happened that made him feel like he was choking. He would start screaming, squirming, and kicking so violently that his cries were heartbreaking.

He was clearly suffering, and we spent hours trying to soothe him. Sometimes, these episodes lasted two to four hours.

I knew newborns required a lot of attention, but Moroni was unlike my other children. I didn't understand why he cried so much. We tried different specialized formulas and bottle types, but his tongue—always out and unusually large—seemed to interfere with the sucking process. He moved it oddly.

When he cried inconsolably, we'd rock him, bathe him, massage him—nothing worked.

One day, after hours of crying, I put him in his stroller. For the first time, he calmed down. That's when we discovered that the stroller was the only thing that brought him comfort.

We spent hours walking around the house with him in it, all while I tried to meet the needs of my other children, who also needed attention.

I felt exhausted and frustrated because I couldn't find peace or encouragement while Moroni cried without end. I recorded many of those episodes, even when he was screaming as I tried to feed him. I did it so I could show doctors and specialists what was happening—because words weren't enough to explain what we were experiencing.

These videos helped show that something was clearly wrong, but the doctors couldn't find a cause. Every week, I went to the ER, showing them the videos. They could see something was off and suspected he was in great pain, but all the tests came back normal—no infections or detectable issues.

It was heartbreaking and discouraging because no one would help him, and I kept coming home with the same problem, not knowing what to do.

I want to share this part of my story because it was one of the greatest manifestations of God's power I've ever experienced. It still pains me to say it—but the truth is: I reached a point where I didn't want Moroni near me. I couldn't bear his cries.

Before my pregnancy with Moroni, I used to post many videos on social media. I had a large community of followers eager to know how my baby and I were doing.

One day, I shared a video of Moroni during one of his crying episodes. That video reached 11 million views and had 16,000 comments.

I was amazed by how many people shared my thoughts: Moroni was in a lot of pain for some unknown reason.

Things weren't getting better, and I desperately wanted to stop feeling the way I did. I felt alone—maybe I wasn't truly alone, but emotionally, I was.

One day, I decided to surrender—to turn to the only One who could free me from those negative feelings, from frustration, impatience, and pain.

I remember kneeling and pouring my soul out to God. I shared my deepest feelings and weaknesses. I begged Him to give me more love, more patience, more empathy—that He would fill my heart with charity toward Moroni, give me the strength to endure his screams and episodes without breaking down, and help me find a way to ease his pain.

I remember praying like that for a few days—and then, something happened.

Moroni didn't stop crying—that continued for years—but I no longer felt that same desperation. I had always been a very impatient person, but I know something changed in me.

When Moroni cried, I felt peace. I experienced deep calm and immense love for him. That connection helped me focus on him rather than on myself. I stopped thinking about how I felt and began to worry about how he felt.

Whenever he had multiple crying episodes each day, I would think: **"What can I do to help this tiny, fragile baby feel calm and comfortable? How can I help him sleep and rest?"**

That's when I began intensely searching online for items, remedies, and techniques to help him. I read about weighted blankets, which help calm the nervous system by applying deep pressure—like a hug—and reduce anxiety and improve sleep.

We also tried different electric swings to soothe him and even hung a manual swing from the ceiling in our bedroom. I experimented with sound and vibration machines.

To this day, I'm amazed at how much love God allowed me to feel. I spent countless hours rocking him or pushing his stroller, never once thinking about myself. I know I couldn't have done it alone. I'm certain that—even though I couldn't see them—angels were holding me up, giving me strength day after day.

I held Moroni with such intensity and love that nothing was more important to me than calming him while I was full of peace and stillness. My heart connected with God. I felt His mercy—and I passed that mercy on to my baby.

In that experience, I gained a powerful testimony: that God gives us love, patience, and charity when we ask for it.

If we cry out to Him with all our hearts, He will help us learn how to manage our emotions.

I gave my heart to God, and He gave me a pure gift—something I didn't have before, a gift I learned to develop day by day. That gift allowed me to help my son heal and live as peacefully as possible.

I never knew a baby could suffer so much—until I met Moroni.

I feel honored to be part of God's love for His children and to be the protector of such a special little soul.

God, through His holy scriptures, invites us to ask Him for everything we need—even the small things we sometimes think are insignificant. But if it matters to us, it matters to Him.

One of my favorite scriptures in the New Testament is:

Matthew 7:7–11

"Ask, and it will be given to you; seek, and you will find; knock, and the door will be opened to you.

For everyone who asks receives; the one who seeks finds; and to the one who knocks, the door will be opened.

Which of you, if your son asks for bread, will give him a stone? Or if he asks for a fish, will give him a snake?

If you, then, though you are evil, know how to give good gifts to your children, how much more will your Father in heaven give good things to those who ask Him!"

It's a beautiful truth—our Heavenly Father wants to bless us. I invite you to start each day by asking God for what you need. Whether it's more patience with your children, a better job, the health of a loved one, hope, guidance through confusion, help on a test, strength to forgive, or the desire to be a parent—there are countless reasons to pray.

I can testify that God hears our prayers. While many people in the world believe God doesn't exist because He doesn't grant everything they ask for, I can assure you that He does bless us—according to what we need.

He often answers in unexpected ways and at a very different time than we expect—but He always answers. The way God responds and blesses us is higher and holier than what we think we need. Let's allow Him to work in our lives as He sees fit.

I know the greatest treasure I can leave my children is the knowledge that God hears and answers our prayers. That knowledge will strengthen their faith.

Life will be filled with high, exhausting mountains—with potholes, bumps, and stones—but if they trust in God, they'll make it.

That's why we pray every day at home—because we need God and His strength to face each day's challenges. Through personal experience, I know that prayer keeps the windows of heaven open over our lives and needs.

When that happens, we will witness the great miracles God performs in our lives.

Prayer is like a bridge that connects us with our Creator.

In our home, we pray this way:

Step 1: We address God as our Heavenly Father.

When we pray, we begin by calling on God as "Heavenly Father." You might have a special way of referring to Him—and that's perfectly okay. What matters is that we come with the desire to talk to Him, as if we were dialing the phone to speak with someone important. Just like you would ask for the person you want to talk to when making a call, in prayer we make sure to address God, who is always ready to listen.

Step 2: We thank Him for the blessings we receive.

Giving thanks is a fundamental part of prayer. Recognizing the blessings God gives us helps us stay humble and remember that everything we are and have is thanks to Him. Expressing gratitude connects us to His love and generosity, and it fills our hearts with thankfulness. God is pleased when we are grateful.

Step 3: We ask Him for the things we need—both for ourselves and for others.

There's nothing too small or too big for our Heavenly Father, because He loves us and wants to help. The Bible teaches us: "Let your requests be made known unto God in every prayer" (Philippians 4:6–7), reminding us that God hears our pleas. When we ask in faith, we trust that He will answer in the way that is best for us—according to His wisdom and love.

Step 4: We end our prayer in the name of Jesus Christ.
We conclude our prayer by saying, "In the name of Jesus Christ, Amen." This is important because Jesus Christ is the only mediator between us and Heavenly Father. He gave His life for us, opened the way for us to draw closer to God, and He is our Savior. Saying Amen at the end means we agree with everything we said in the prayer and that we trust God will hear and respond.

Prayer is an intimate and special conversation with the Father. We approach it with reverence, respect, and love. We try not to pray hastily or repeat the same words. Instead, we reflect in our hearts on what we truly need, and above all, we treasure the blessings we've received.

In the following chapters, I will continue talking about prayer, as it has been present in all our experiences. I will share how God has answered our prayers in ways we didn't expect—and that, at times, were very difficult for me to accept.

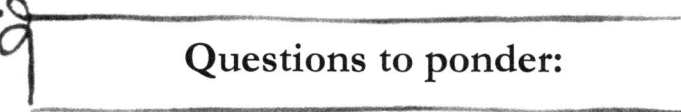

Questions to ponder:

1. How can I improve my daily communication with God?

2. Am I taking time to give thanks before asking for things?

3. What obstacles are keeping me from praying more often or more sincerely?

4. How can I invite the Holy Ghost to guide my prayers?

Steps to take action:

1. Create a daily prayer schedule:
Set aside a specific time in the morning, during the day, or at night to talk with God. Even just a few minutes a day can make a big difference.

2. Pray with gratitude:
Make a list of at least three things you're thankful for before you begin your prayer. This will help you focus on the positive.

3. Pray for others:
Think of someone who needs help or comfort, and pray specifically for them.

4. Find a quiet place:
Choose a special space where you can be calm and focus on your communication with God.

CHAPTER 2

FAITH TO ACCEPT NOT BEING HEALED

"Now faith is the substance of things
hoped for, the evidence of things not
seen."

- Hebrews 11:1

You've probably heard the phrase that compares prayer to carrying an umbrella. When someone prays for rain and does so with faith, they are so certain it will rain that they bring an umbrella—ready to stay dry when it does. That kind of confidence in God's power to work miracles is beautiful.

In recent years, however, I've learned a new aspect of faith: There is also faith to accept not being healed. I know that God has the power to do anything and move any mountain. But what if He chooses not to do it for me? Will I still worship Him? Will I continue to trust in His wisdom, His love, and His mercy?

If what I ask for is not granted, will I turn away from Him? Will I blame Him, reject His counsel, and distance myself because I didn't get what I thought I needed? Or will I accept His will and stay close to Him?

This deeper understanding of faith came to me through pain and experience. And because of it, I have been able to follow the Lord with a more grounded, resilient faith.

Let's return to the umbrella example: the person who prayed for rain believed it would come. They were prepared, pulled out their umbrella, and waited in hope. But the rain never came. Was their faith in vain?

Here is where a deeper, transformative type of faith comes in: faith to accept God's will. This kind of faith is not only about believing God can do what we ask, but also trusting that His will—whatever it may be—is perfect. It means accepting His decisions with humility and strength, even when they don't match our desires.

The person who believed in the rain didn't give up when it didn't fall. Instead, they got buckets, filled them from their shower, and watered the flowers themselves. They didn't let the absence of rain crush their hope. They acted with courage and trust, knowing God's will is always good—even when we don't understand it.

This is the kind of faith that transforms us. The kind that helps us move forward even when our prayers aren't answered the way we hoped. It's the faith that motivates us to do our part, to be instruments in God's hands, and to find purpose in the process.

That is the topic I want to address in this chapter: having a **"faith to accept not being healed."** I heard this phrase in a talk by Elder David A. Bednar, and it changed the way I understand faith.

Moroni faced one health issue after another. It was obvious that things were not okay. Many people approached me saying, **"You just need more faith,"** or **"If you pray with more faith, believing that God can do everything..."** Some even said, **"I think you're lacking faith."**

Those words hurt deeply, as if my son wasn't being healed because I didn't have enough faith. But they were wrong. God has healed my son—in His own time. He didn't take away his conditions, and Moroni has had to endure a great deal of pain and hardship. But the faith to accept God's will, even when it means not being healed or even facing the possibility of death, gave me a peace I cannot explain. It helped me find calm and trust Him completely.

When Moroni was around two months old, during a hospital visit, the doctors found a heart murmur. The doctor said there was no immediate cause for alarm, but that we should return in a month to see a cardiologist. At three months old, we returned. The cardiologist ran detailed exams and ultrasounds of Moroni's heart.

When he came back into the room, he told me Moroni's arteries were extremely small and that his heart wasn't pumping blood properly—he was dying.

He explained that the only known cause for such a serious condition was Williams syndrome.

The doctor stepped out, and I quickly Googled **"Williams syndrome."** When I saw photos of children with it, I felt something strange—almost a sense of relief: Moroni looked just like them. He had the same bright eyes, the same nose, the same smile.

As the cardiologist had said, one of the main complications of Williams syndrome is congenital heart disease. Not every child with the syndrome has heart problems, but Moroni did.

Suddenly, I understood why he cried so much—he wasn't just struggling with his heart. He was also hypersensitive to sound (hyperacusis), and had both over- and under-sensitivities in different parts of his body, along with severe gastrointestinal issues.

The cardiologist told me Moroni wouldn't survive more than three months without heart surgery. That day was devastating. I wasn't expecting such news. I had gone to the appointment alone.

When I got home, my husband and I cried. The pain was so deep, I couldn't get out of bed for two days. But then I prayed—and in that process, I found the strength to get up again. I had two other children who needed their mother. I had been completely paralyzed by grief.

After some time reflecting, I knelt and prayed: **"My Father, thank You for giving me four months with Moroni. Thank You for letting me hold him, kiss him, and get to know him. He is my son, and You gave him to me as a gift.**

Now I give him back to You. He is Yours. You loaned him to me. If You decide to take him back, I will accept it. I trust that You have a magnificent plan for him. Do with him what You will.

Just please give me strength to endure this pain and find peace. Give me courage to not complain. Whether he lives or dies, he is Yours, and I trust Your will. You are a perfect God, and I place my son in Your hands."

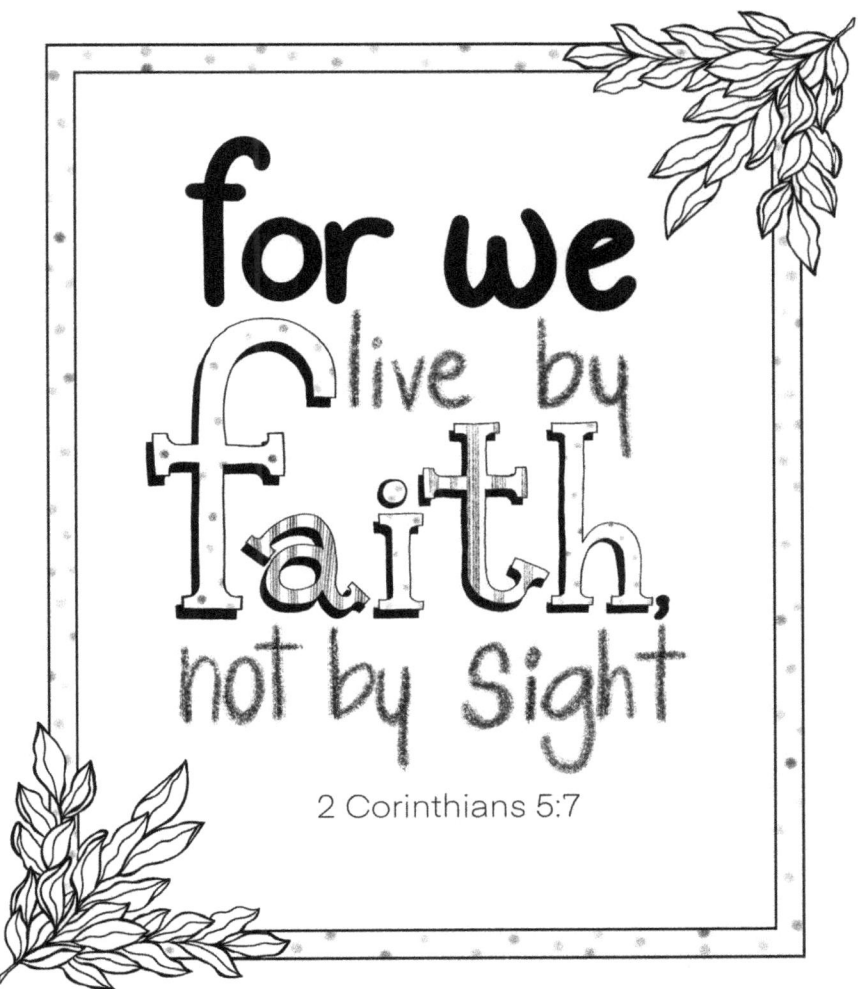

for we live by faith, not by sight

2 Corinthians 5:7

As soon as I finished praying, I felt an incredible sense of relief. The worst thing that could happen—losing my child—no longer frightened me. I trusted that if he returned to his Heavenly Father, it would be to a place free from pain.

Moroni had already suffered so much. I knew one day we would be together again. From that moment on, I stopped worrying. I chose to have faith to accept God's will.

A few weeks passed while we waited for the call to schedule the surgery. The procedure required a specialized team to come from another hospital because Moroni was at high risk if the wrong anesthesia was used due to his syndrome. A cardiothoracic anesthesiology team was needed; the surgery would be highly invasive.

After a few weeks, I finally got the call. We were scheduled to come to the hospital to go over the process and details of Moroni's surgery.

That day arrived, and we were incredibly nervous. The surgeon's assistant began explaining step by step what would happen to Moroni. There was so much information that I only remember bits and pieces. She sounded astonished and mentioned that Children's Health in Dallas hadn't performed an open-heart surgery as extensive as Moroni's in over ten years. They were planning to repair all the arteries in his heart.

She explained they would make a vertical incision in his chest, break his sternum, and spread his ribs apart. Once the cuts were made, they would open his chest like a book. Then, they would remove all his blood and run it through machines, freezing his heart while they reconstructed the arteries using a mesh—like chicken wire but much smaller and made of different material.

After the procedure, they would unfreeze his heart, and that moment would be the most critical—the moment they would wait to see if his heart would beat again.

That would be the true miracle.

If the heart didn't respond, they would attempt to resuscitate him. And if that still didn't work, they would connect him to a machine called ECMO, which would temporarily function as his heart. I can't describe the feelings that overcame us in that moment.

With so much uncertainty and faith, we signed the consent forms, returned home, and spent the following weeks preparing for what was to come.

A few days before the open-heart surgery, we asked all our family to come visit Moroni and take pictures with him, knowing there was a chance he might not survive. It was an incredibly emotional moment.

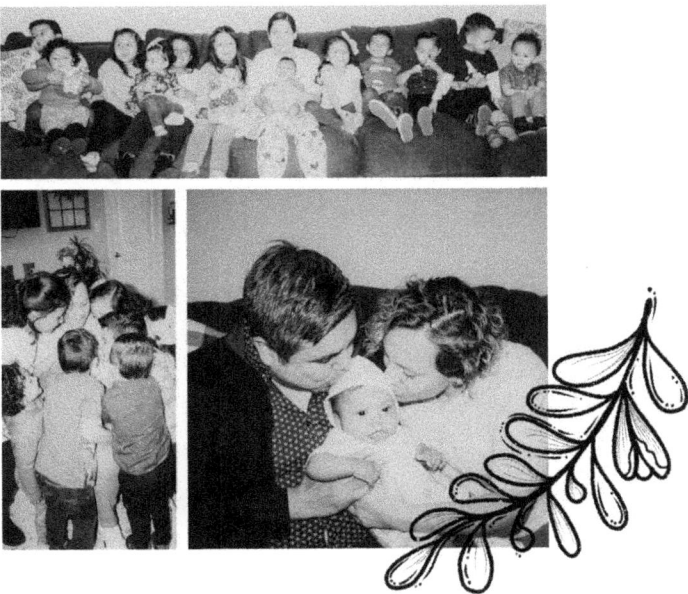

The night before the surgery, all five of us—my husband, our three children, and I—slept in the same bed, taking turns cuddling Moroni. I wanted that moment to last forever. I leaned close to his little face to feel his breath. I touched every part of his body to feel his skin, as if trying to memorize his scent and essence, never wanting to forget them.

The day of the surgery finally came. As they took Moroni from the room, it felt like my heart was being ripped from my chest, knowing it might be the last time I'd see him alive.

But my husband and I remembered our conversation with God, and He gave us strength. As the hours passed, we began to feel peace, courage, and—surprisingly—joy. I can't explain the serenity we felt. There was no reason to cry, because we knew everything was in God's hands. And death, after all, is the door that brings us back into the presence of our Father. We had accepted that this, too, was part of His plan.

During the entire process, we continued praying and giving our hearts to God. After ten long hours, my phone rang. My heart was pounding. It was a nurse. She excitedly told us that Moroni's heart was beating again.

We still had to wait two more hours to see him, but we no longer had to worry—God had fulfilled His perfect will.

That day, the heavens opened. Miracles were manifested. A broken body was healed, and a sleeping heart beat strong again. Arms were lifted, hearts were filled with hope, and tears turned into joy.

Negative diagnoses were overcome. Angels ministered. And the power of God was visible every minute, every hour.

That day, my son Moroni was lifted, strengthened, and healed. God worked miracles and showed us that Moroni had a purpose on this earth—not only to strengthen his family but to show the world that God lives, that He loves us, hears us, and helps us.

When we walked into the room where Moroni was lying, it was overwhelming to see his small body in such a condition. Tubes filled with blood came from his stomach and other parts of his body. He was connected to wires from head to toe—with IVs in both arms, his neck, his foot, and leg, and tubes in his stomach, nose, and mouth.

It was a terrifying scene. The room was filled with machines that beeped constantly, each playing a crucial role in keeping my child alive.

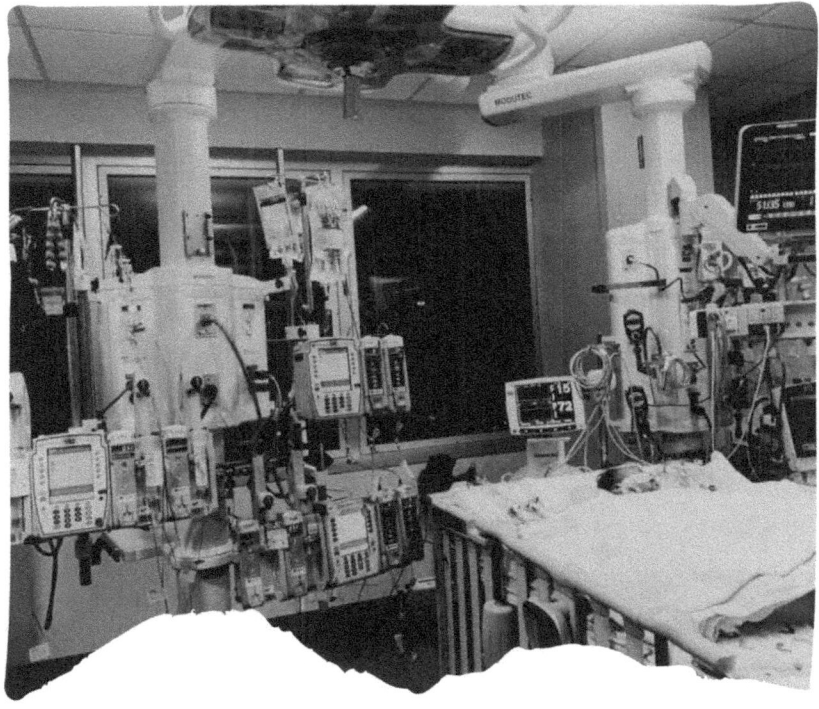

No mother should ever have to see her child in the condition I saw mine. It was as if he were dead. And he remained like that for several days. They were dark days—days I never imagined I would experience.

I know God could have healed my son in an instant—with a single word. He could have completely restored his body. But He chose a different path. He chose to work through specialists, through the hands of surgeons, and through medical technology. And all of this—guided by His love and wisdom—became a great miracle.

God did not remove Moroni's pain. His body was cut, wounded, and marked by multiple procedures. He spent three weeks in intensive care. Initially, we were told it would only be a few days.

His recovery was slow and filled with extremely difficult moments. Every time they tried to remove the breathing tubes, his lungs wouldn't take in oxygen properly. He suffered respiratory failure several times, and each time, his chest wounds reopened.

They tried two more times, unsuccessfully. He was taken back to the OR so they could find out why his lungs were collapsing. Eventually, they decided to try a different gas called heliox, which is easier to breathe. He also went through episodes of hypothermia.

God didn't shield us from any of that pain—not for him, nor for us as parents. We cried a lot. And due to COVID-19 restrictions, we cried alone—my husband and I weren't allowed to be in the hospital together.

At home, I had two other children who needed their mom. They struggled with depression due to the drastic changes in our lives, and my heart ached from everything I was witnessing.

There were moments when the doctors and nurses informed me that something wasn't going well. In those moments, I had to stay strong—not scream or cry in front of them—because I didn't want them to see me fall apart.

So, I would go into the bathroom—where I knew I could let it out unseen. There, through silent sobs, I would try to release the weight of the emotions that consumed me.

Many times, I truly felt like I couldn't bear any more pain. God didn't spare us from any of it. Why? I don't know.

But what I do know is this: I came to know deep sorrow—and at the same time, profound joy. Because the small miracles that came, day by day, during Moroni's recovery were divine.

I felt the strength of my Heavenly Father, who showed me His goodness in unexpected ways. In my hardest moments, when I felt I couldn't take another step, I knew He walked with me. I felt His hand holding me, filling me with peace.

Though I was physically alone, I was never truly alone— His presence was real in my life. God cared. He taught me to be strong—physically and emotionally.

He gave me the ability to care for Moroni and to stay alert to his needs, even though I had no medical experience. He helped me recognize when something was wrong and gave me the words and courage to speak with nurses and doctors in English.

He helped me defend my son's rights and make sure he was cared for in the unique way he needed. Moroni was extremely sensitive, and his constant crying was heartbreaking. Many times, I had to beg or even demand more pain medicine for him. Though nurses had strict schedules for medication, I felt the courage to insist when necessary.

I also demanded that no one enter the room to perform tests—like bloodwork or X-rays—without my consent. Only I, as his mother, knew when the time was right. And though that meant some specialists had to wait hours to return, I did it all for Moroni's well-being.

I also asked that he not be bathed daily, and even diaper changes had to be done gently. Moroni used cloth diapers for over a year, and at the hospital it was very difficult to clean them, but I did it all out of love for him.

Some may say I was extreme, but I didn't do it for myself—I did it for my baby. So, he could rest peacefully as much as possible. Because I knew that otherwise, he'd suffer more crying and discomfort.

Each doctor who cared for Moroni was amazed at how involved I was with his health and how I advocated for him. One of the doctors even asked me if I had medical training because of how responsibly I handled everything.

God gave Moroni the strength to overcome the pain, to endure the needles, and to face everything that came his way. Little by little, he started drinking again from his bottle.

Moroni began to regain strength, and with his tiny hands, he grabbed my fingers again.

One day, I was feeling sad, watching old videos to remember how joyful and full of life my son used to be. Tears streamed down my face. Somehow, my husband sensed my sorrow. He called me and said he would stay with Moroni that afternoon so I could go home to be with our other kids and rest.

When I came back to the hospital, I couldn't believe my eyes—Moroni no longer had any IVs or breathing tubes!

As I spoke with the nurse, trying to process what I was seeing, Moroni looked at me, and with his usual tenderness, he smiled at me and began to babble.

That moment was a gift from heaven—a light-filled moment I will treasure in my heart forever.

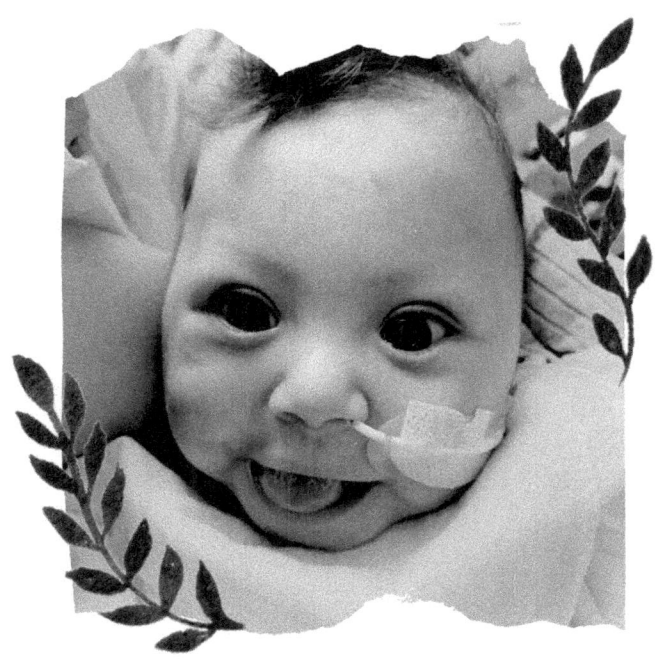

During that process, we met nurses whom I deeply admire and for whom I feel immense gratitude. With great kindness, they stayed with me through the early hours of the morning, gently rocking Moroni's crib with dedication and patience.

To this day, I am still amazed by the kindness of many of them. As his mother, I didn't mind standing for four hours in the middle of the night rocking his crib—but many of them did it for me. Some even held his pacifier in place with their finger because he didn't have the strength to keep it in his mouth. To bring him comfort, we would hold it for him.

It was in those moments that my son revealed one of his most admirable qualities: his resilience. His ability to face challenges and his unbreakable spirit reflected God's power and love working in his life.

Jesus healed the sick, gave sight to the blind, and made the lame walk. However, not everyone was healed while Jesus walked the earth. Still, many people—burdened, sad, discouraged, and ill—did not receive physical healing. But Jesus showed us something greater: the path to spiritual and emotional strength. Through His example and teachings, He gave us the tools and the power to face and overcome anything in this life, reminding us of that faith in Him is enough to get through any adversity.

Moroni's syndrome has no cure—it will not go away, and that's okay. His syndrome is a demonstration of God's love. Even though there is no cure, God has helped my son overcome many diagnoses, and though the journey has been painful, he has conquered challenges we never imagined.

Moroni's life is perfectly imperfect.

All things are POSSIBLE to him who BELIEVES

Mark 9:23

How is it possible that, during chaos and pain, we can find such deep satisfaction, joy, and hope? That is only possible through the guiding and comforting light of Jesus Christ.

My son survived, and I know there are many babies, children, teens, and adults who have departed this world. But that doesn't mean God is unfair or that He loves Moroni more.

If we could only see beyond this world—if the veil were lifted from our eyes—we would understand that death is simply another step toward our heavenly home. We are on this earth for a limited time—a time designed for us to have experiences that bring knowledge, strength, and preparation for what comes when we pass to the other side of the veil.

I am convinced that one day we will see again those we love who passed before us. We will see them, embrace them, and remember our earthly experiences together. And they will tell us that they were always by our side, watching over us with infinite love.

That day will be glorious—full of love, joy, and endless peace. It will be a moment free of illness, sorrow, worry, and pain.

There, we will clearly understand that all our experiences—even the hardest ones—were necessary for our growth. We will thank Jesus Christ for His infinite love and for His willingness to give His life so that we could all have the chance to return to our Heavenly Father and our families.

For now, we must hold on to trust, confidence, and faith in God that this day will come. Though from our earthly perspective it may seem far away, in God's time, it is much closer than we can imagine.

Walking toward God with faith is like moving forward blindfolded while hearing His voice asking you to keep going. You know there's a cliff nearby, but you don't stop; you take steady steps because you trust that He has placed an invisible bridge that is only revealed to those who believe in Him.

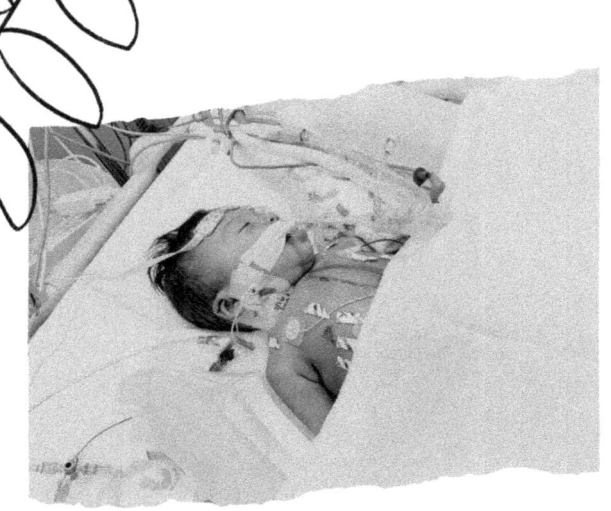

A difficult day, but filled with hope: the day of the surgery.

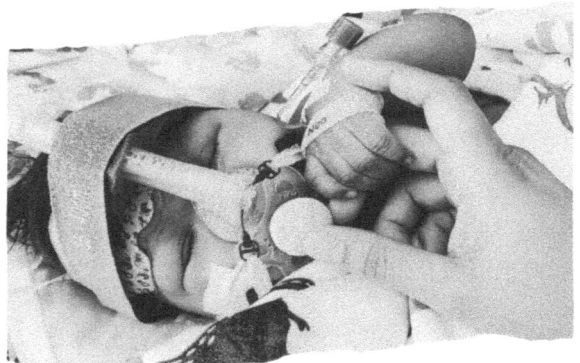

One day at a time: in recovery.

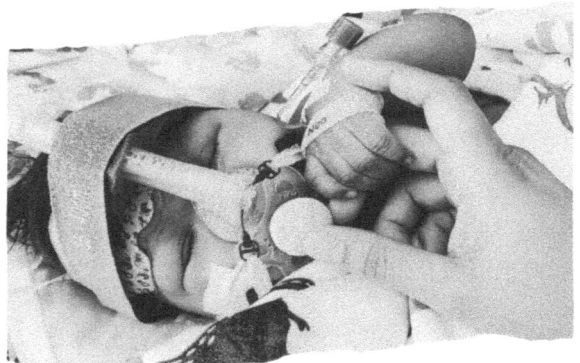

After the battle, the victory: the day he left the hospital.

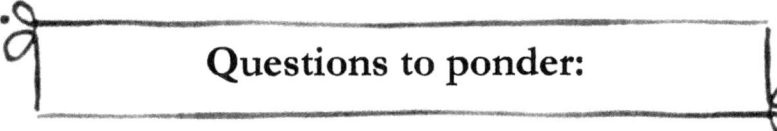
Questions to ponder:

1. What experiences have I lived through where my faith was tested, and I learned something valuable from them?

2. Am I truly willing to surrender my desires and accept God's will, even when it's different from what I hope for?

3. What invisible or unexpected miracles have I received during my trials that I may not have recognized before?

Steps to take action:

1. Make a list of difficult moments
Reflect on how those experiences helped you grow spiritually and thank God for the lessons you've learned.

2. Write a prayer of surrender
Take time to write a personal prayer in which you entrust your desires and fears to God, expressing your willingness to accept His will.

3. Read faith stories from the Bible
Study the lives of people who trusted God, like Job, Joseph of Egypt, or Paul. Let their journeys strengthen your own faith.

4. Write your own "faith testimony"
Reflect on how God has guided you in the past and write about it to solidify your trust in His plan.

5. Identify what you can control
Make a list of actions that are within your power to take in faith and surrender to God the things that are outside your control.

6. Pray specifically for acceptance

Dedicate some prayers to asking God for strength and peace to accept His will for your life.

7. Surround your life with visual reminders

Place scriptures, quotes, or images where you'll see them often—reminders to trust in God's perfect plan.

CHAPTER 3

PERSONAL REVELATION

"If any of you lack wisdom, let him ask
of God, that giveth to all men liberally,
and upbraideth not; and it shall be given
him."

- James 1:5

J ust as it is important to pray to God and ask for all the things
we need, it is also essential to learn how to recognize when and
how He answers us. God does answer our prayers, but we need to
be attentive and open to discern His responses. Beyond asking, we
must learn to listen and understand what He wants us to do.

Personal revelation is that special connection through which
God guides us, comforts us, and shows us the way, revealing His
will for our lives.

From birth, Moroni always had his tongue out. As I mentioned
before, I often asked doctors why my son constantly had his tongue
out, but no one ever gave me an answer.

Every specialist I saw—his dentist, pediatrician, geneticist, gastroenterologist, and every other professional—couldn't explain why Moroni's tongue was so large or why he couldn't keep it inside his mouth. I decided to trust them and give them the time they asked for, as they told me that as his head grew, his mouth would become large enough to hold his tongue.

I accepted their advice, but I constantly asked God to guide me and show me how I could help Moroni, because he had serious difficulties with feeding. Milk would spill out the sides of his mouth, and I was never able to breastfeed him because of his low muscle tone, swallowing, sucking, pressing, and moving his tongue were all extremely difficult for him.

With his tongue constantly out, Moroni drooled excessively. I remember making special bibs with my mom, adding waterproof fabric so his chest wouldn't be soaked, as he began developing sores on his neck from all the saliva that built up.

But that wasn't all—he also choked and coughed frequently. His tongue caused him a lot of discomfort, and as parents, it was painful for us to see him so uncomfortable.

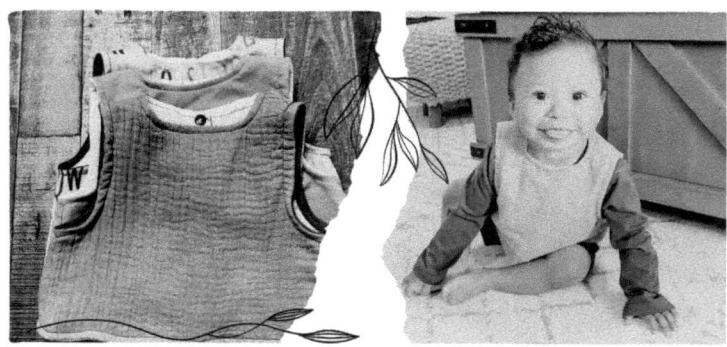

I felt immense helplessness at not having a clear answer on how to help my son. But something deep inside me kept saying that there had to be a solution for Moroni, even if we didn't know what it was yet.

I found a specialized therapy for saliva control, and Moroni attended for a few months, but we didn't get the results we hoped for. He was extremely sensitive—no one could touch his mouth or even get close to his face without him crying intensely. In fact, Moroni never put anything in his mouth, something babies do instinctively. He rejected any object brought nearby. This might have been because he had been intubated from birth and later had surgeries that required multiple procedures on his face.

The need to keep searching was constant, and many times I begged God to help me know what to do. Moroni was about to turn two. During that whole time, I had been seeking answers—even though I didn't really know what I was looking for.

One night, around four in the morning, I woke up after hearing a voice. It wasn't an audible voice but rather something that resonated deeply in my mind—a powerful impression. The voice said: **"Search."**

I tried to ignore it, since at the time I barely slept. Even though Moroni was already two years old, caring for him was like caring for a newborn, and I was constantly exhausted.

But again, I heard the word: **"Search."** Despite the extreme fatigue, I could feel the voice's clarity and strength—not as a shout, but firm. This time, I decided to listen. I remember my laptop was right next to my bed. I opened it and sat on the edge of the bed. I didn't know what to do, but something inside me pushed

I will instruct thee and teach thee in the way which thou shalt go: I will guide thee with mine eye.

Psalm 32:8

me to begin searching. I started typing into Google and YouTube using keywords like **"large tongue," "Williams syndrome,"** and **"excessive drooling."** I was determined to find an answer.

After an hour of searching, I found a video on YouTube. Today, with all the technology and advancements we have, it's easier to access important information. Of course, we must be careful and avoid self-diagnosing based on what we find online. It's essential to use good judgment and seek qualified specialists who can confirm or rule out any diagnosis.

In the video, a doctor was talking about **Beckwith-Wiedemann syndrome**, a genetic condition where one of its features is **macroglossia,** or a very large tongue. Although that wasn't Moroni's condition, I decided to watch the entire video.

In that video, the doctor said something that struck me deeply. He said: **"I'm against so many specialists telling families that the child will grow, and the mouth will get bigger, and eventually the tongue will fit. I don't understand why they say that, because with a simple tongue-reduction surgery, you can change a child's quality of life."**

When I heard those words, my heart was filled with hope. They were exactly the same words I had been told by the specialists I had consulted.

I felt that God, through the Holy Ghost, had guided me and spoken to me through that video and through that doctor. It wasn't God coming to tell me directly what I needed to know, but through that social media platform, I received crucial information that made all the difference.

God answers our prayers and speaks to us with a still, small voice. It's a voice we feel in our hearts and understand in our minds. But in our daily lives, we are often so busy, so surrounded by noise and distractions, that we don't allow God the space to speak to us. It becomes difficult to hear the soft whisper of His Spirit.

That's why I believe God spoke to me at 4 a.m. He knew my days were filled with stress, responsibilities, and worries, so He chose a time when I would be more still—when He knew I would hear Him.

That doesn't mean we can only hear Him at that hour—God can speak to us anytime—we just need to be in tune with Him.

For me, knowing I had finally found a solution to my son's problem was wonderful, but I didn't expect that the road ahead would cost us so many tears.

1 Kings 19:11–12
"And he said, Go forth, and stand upon the mount before the Lord. And, behold, the Lord passed by, and a great and strong wind rent the mountains, and brake in pieces the rocks before the Lord; but the Lord was not in the wind: and after the wind an earthquake; but the Lord was not in the earthquake: And after the earthquake a fire; but the Lord was not in the fire: and after the fire a still small voice."

When God Speaks, We Obey

It was a Sunday when I saw the video about tongue-reduction surgery, and not many specialists usually work on that day. I waited until it was around nine in the morning and called the hospital in Miami, the one mentioned in the video.

To my surprise, someone answered. They explained that, at that hospital, before performing the surgery, a full team of specialists evaluates the child's tongue and mouth to determine whether the procedure is truly necessary.

That caught my attention, so I asked if I could schedule an appointment. I was determined to travel to Miami no matter the effort—anything to help my son.

However, when I gave them my personal information and address, the person said, **"I don't think you need to come all the way here. There's a very well-known and excellent craniofacial surgeon in Dallas—Dr. Jeffrey Fearon. I can give you his contact information."**

She passed along his details, and to me, that was another miracle. I received very valuable information—and on a Sunday. The fact that I didn't need to travel to Miami but that there was a local specialist was truly a blessing.

A few days later, I scheduled an appointment with him, but it wouldn't be for another two months. Since I now knew what kind of medical specialty could help, I decided to look for another craniofacial surgeon to see if I could get an earlier appointment.

Surprisingly, I got one very quickly. I remember thinking it was strange that it was so soon, but I went right away.

At that appointment, I met with another craniofacial surgeon and explained Moroni's entire history—how he had struggled to eat and his excessive drooling. I even mentioned that, during a dental X-ray, it had been seen that Moroni's teeth were beginning to shift outward due to the pressure of his tongue.

After hearing everything, the doctor did not recommend surgery. According to him, the only reason to do tongue-reduction surgery would be if, as Moroni got older, he was teased, and it began to affect his self-esteem.

We left that appointment very sad and discouraged. Once again, it felt like we hadn't found a solution. At that point, I decided to stop searching and simply do my part as his mom: to keep helping him however I could.

The next day, I called Dr. Fearon's office to cancel the appointment, thinking I had already received a professional opinion. But the person who answered encouraged me to reconsider, suggesting that getting a second opinion might be worth it. I decided to follow that advice.

Finally, the day arrived, and I was able to explain everything to Dr. Fearon—including the fact that I had already consulted another surgeon. When he heard this, Dr. Fearon seemed shocked and surprised by what I'd been told. He told me that, in his opinion, it was obvious that Moroni needed tongue-reduction surgery, and that he could perform it.

We finally scheduled the surgery. Moroni had the procedure done at Medical City Children's Hospital. When I saw my son after the surgery, I couldn't hold back my tears. I apologized to him for everything he had been through. What I saw was heartbreaking—it

Blessed rather are those who hear the word of God and Obey it.

Luke 11:28

looked as though his entire tongue had been removed, or as if he no longer had a tongue at all. But it was still there—it was just so swollen, like a round ball, and that terrified me.

I felt regret and guilt; an overwhelming heaviness invaded my thoughts. I started wondering if I had gone too far—if I had lost control trying to fix something that couldn't be fixed. I truly felt lost.

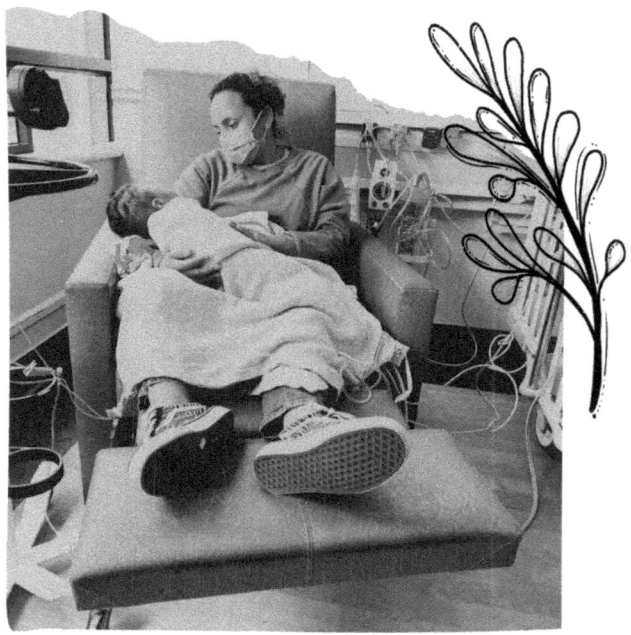

Even though the surgeon had told us it would be a simple procedure and that Moroni would be eating again in five days, we've come to understand that he is very different from other children—his recovery and learning would go take more time.

The surgery was extremely aggressive for him and incredibly difficult to endure. Moroni ended up staying in the hospital three weeks, when originally it had only been planned for two days.

His recovery was complicated. It was as if he had become a newborn all over again—or even worse, because he couldn't even drink milk from a bottle.

I felt discouraged. We had worked so hard to help him learn how to eat better, and it felt like all that effort had been thrown away. So many hours of therapy wasted. All the time invested in helping him swallow better, take his bottle, and bring things to his mouth... everything we had gained suddenly vanished.

Everyone at home was deeply affected by seeing him unable to eat like before. When we offered him his bottle, he rejected it, and after many tries, when he finally took it, the milk spilled out the sides of his mouth. It was alarming—he cried and fussed non-stop.

In the end, it became necessary to place a nasogastric tube, as he couldn't use the bottle. But since it was only supposed to be temporary, the doctor didn't provide a specialized feeding machine—we had to do it manually. We elevated the tube to let gravity help the milk flow, and with a large syringe, we would slowly push it in.

My husband and I felt anxious and stressed every single time it was time to feed him through the tube, because we knew it would be a terrifying process full of screams. Moroni could feel the milk passing through the tube, and it scared him. We're not exactly sure why, but the feeling of the milk moving through his nose, esophagus, and stomach was simply too much for him.

His recovery was very slow, completely different from what the surgeon had told us. But once again, we were reminded: Moroni is unique.

This process was also extremely hard on our other children. Watching their little brother suffer scared them and filled them with worry. And emotionally, it was hard for them not to have mom and dad available like before. I couldn't take them to their classes, or play with them, or read them stories the way I used to. Even though I tried to give them quality time, the reality was that balancing everything was incredibly difficult.

One afternoon, while Moroni was sitting down, he somehow pulled the tube out of his nose completely. We decided to take him to a nearby hospital.

When we arrived, they told us they couldn't replace the tube because they only had nasogastric tubes for adults. The same thing happened at two other nearby hospitals. We were deeply concerned because Moroni needed to be fed every three hours, and the longer he went without eating, the more likely he would get hungry and begin one of his intense crying episodes.

Finally, we decided to take him to his usual hospital, where we waited six long hours until they were able to insert the tube again. We got home around three in the morning, completely exhausted.

But around five in the morning, my husband Jorge noticed something strange—the tube was wrapped around Moroni's neck, and it was no longer in his nose.

Filled with worry, he woke me up yelling, **"Gabby, the tube came out again!"**

The frustration was overwhelming. This time, Jorge decided to take Moroni to the hospital by himself while I stayed home with the other kids. That night was extremely stressful and exhausting—physically, mentally, and emotionally. Moroni was dealing with so many health problems, and because he has congenital heart conditions and Williams syndrome, he was at risk of dehydration, which could affect his heart. So many fears ran through our minds.

When We Obey His Voice, We Receive Blessings

During that month of recovery, I felt how God comforted me and helped me develop new skills—like feeding my son through a nasogastric tube. I learned to insert the tube in his nose, check if it was properly placed in the stomach, apply and remove adhesive without hurting him, and even invented a way to clip the tube to prevent it from tangling. This made our lives a bit easier.

When it was time to feed him, everyone at home joined in to sing, cheer him up, and distract him before the milk began flowing through the tube. It truly became a team effort.

God also helped me develop more patience and showed me that, even when we have to start from zero, we can reach our goals again. We felt His presence in our home, near Moroni and our other children, and we felt His love through people who called just to lift our spirits.

When the Holy Spirit speaks to us, His guidance fills us with heavenly wisdom.

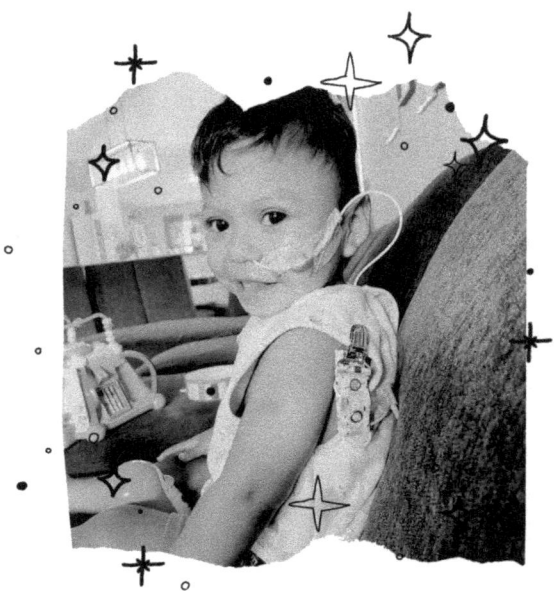

I obeyed God's voice by searching as He prompted me to. I followed His direction and made sure Moroni got that surgery. But the path wasn't easy—and it rarely is.

There will be times when obeying His voice and commandments leads to an easier life, and solutions arrive quickly. But if you have obeyed and feel like everything is getting harder, don't stop believing. Trust in God's timing and His perfect plan for you—a plan designed to help you develop new skills, strengthen your unique gifts, and gain deeper understanding.

Personal growth requires overcoming obstacles, because each challenge is an opportunity to grow in every area of life. Don't give up. Keep a grateful heart and a positive mindset, because God will never abandon you. He will lift you and help you move forward. And when you do, you won't be the same person—you'll be stronger, more resilient, and filled with deeper compassion for others.

Little by little, with the help of his therapist, Moroni began drinking milk from a bottle again. Then he started eating purées and chewing more solid textures. These were beautiful, grateful moments—true miracles that showed me that with perseverance and love, anything is possible.

I shared his progress every day on social media, and it encouraged hundreds of people. Through Moroni's challenges, many people around the world came to witness that God is real and His presence is evident in our lives.

In the end, Moroni reached the same stage he was at before the surgery and continued with therapy, which helped tremendously.

We could see a remarkable change in his face: he looked different, the drooling had stopped, and we could now fully appreciate his smile and tiny teeth.

One of the greatest blessings from this difficult journey was witnessing how Abby and Mahonri developed deep empathy for their brother.

Today, Moroni is older, and I can clearly see the kindness, love, patience, and compassion Abby and Mahonri have for him. I'm amazed at how excited they get about his smallest achievements. They celebrate every milestone, no matter how small, and see it as a blessing.

This perspective has made them more grateful and aware of daily miracles. Though it was a hard process for them, it also became an experience full of learning, emotional growth, and spiritual strength. I'm sure the lessons they learned will stay with them forever and help them become better human beings.

It deeply touches my heart to hear their prayers, always asking for their brother's well-being. What fills my soul with joy is knowing what they carry in their hearts and what their greatest desires are.

I've had several conversations with Mahonri, who is seven years old. In one of them, he told me about a wish he had. I thought it would be something typical for a child—like lots of money or toys. But his answer left me speechless: **"Of course not, Mom! Don't you know that what I want most is to be able to talk with Moroni?"**

On another occasion, while we were stargazing, Mahonri told me we could make a wish on a star. I watched him close his eyes with such sincere hope, and when he opened them, I asked, **"What did you wish for?"** Once again, he responded: **"Mom, I'm wishing that Moroni can talk."**

I'm deeply grateful to witness God's love reflected in Abby and Mahonri's charitable acts toward their brother. They include him in their games with other kids, guide him, hold his hand so he doesn't fall, share even their most treasured things with him, comfort him, and protect him.

They've developed the same sense of responsibility I feel: to make sure Moroni has a beautiful life. And these challenges haven't only impacted me, Jorge, Abby, and Mahonri—they've touched my whole family, especially my wonderful nieces and nephews.

Moroni is blessed with 11 cousins who live nearby. He's the youngest of them all, but he has a cousin just one month older than him. It fills me with joy to see how my niece Alice lights up when we visit. She gently places her hands on Moroni's cheeks, looks him in the eyes, and holds his hand so they can play together.

My oldest niece, Regina (16 years old), holds him, hugs him, helps him, and plays with him. Every Sunday at church, Moroni runs to the pew where my older brother's family sits, and my niece Zuheivy—so full of tenderness and patience—holds him so he can sit reverently. She strokes his head and face, calming him.

I can't name all my nieces and nephews here, but each of them runs to greet Moroni when they see him. Their love is so pure and beautiful—and for us, it's a treasure.

One of the most tangible blessings from obeying God's voice in seeking help for my son was this: Moroni had serious trouble sleeping. He moved constantly in his sleep, and at first, doctors thought it was due to low iron levels. He was referred to a sleep specialist.

After spending a night at a sleep lab, Moroni was finally diagnosed with central and obstructive sleep apnea. Central apnea occurs when the part of the brain that controls breathing doesn't function properly, while obstructive apnea is caused by blocked airways—there simply isn't enough space for the air to flow correctly.

During the consultation, while we were going over all of Moroni's diagnoses, the doctor asked if there was anything else to add to his medical history. I mentioned the tongue-reduction surgery, which she hadn't seen in his records since it had been done at a different hospital.

And there it was—a moment of light. The clear answer we had been waiting for. The doctor said it was one of the best decisions we could've made. She explained that had Moroni not undergone that surgery, he would've had serious trouble breathing while asleep.

When she said that, I felt profound relief and joy, knowing that all my son's suffering had not been in vain. It was a clear affirmation that God had answered my prayers and led me to keep searching. He Himself says: **"Seek and you will find."** And I found the specialist my son needed to reduce the size of his tongue, which had caused so many problems.

Today, Moroni still has sleep apnea—but it's not severe; it's moderate. About a year and a half ago, he had to undergo another surgery to remove a small tumor in his airways and to possibly remove his adenoids and tonsils. But the surgeon decided not to remove anything because the procedure might be too aggressive for him.

And once again, the story repeated itself: he was expected to be hospitalized for two nights, but he ended up staying for several weeks and once again needed a nasogastric tube.

We went through the same moments again—but this time with a powerful lesson already learned. With trust, patience, and time, Moroni recovered and went back to using his bottle.

Since that option didn't help him long-term, Moroni now has a CPAP machine—but he hasn't been able to tolerate it yet due to his sensitivity. Still, Moroni is the first to wake up every morning and is always full of energy.

Psalm 84:10–11
"For a day in thy courts is better than a thousand. I
had rather be a doorkeeper in the house of my God,
than to dwell in the tents of wickedness.
For the Lord God is a sun and shield: the Lord will
give grace and glory: no good thing will he withhold
from them that walk uprightly."

"The joy we feel has little to do with the
circumstances of our lives and everything to do with the focus of our lives."

- Russell M. Nelson

If I had lived this experience with Moroni without turning to God, we would not have made it. I would have felt desperate, anxious, bitter—even angry with my son for everything we had to do for him. But with God, everything was easier.

Having Him in our life changes everything—because it changes our focus. My focus was always on God. I kept Him in my mind and heart, and He gave strength to me, to Moroni, and to our family—to move forward with joy and gratitude.

For whoever
wants to save
their life will lose
it, but whoever loses
their life for me
will find it

Matthew 16:25

Questions to ponder:

1. How can I better recognize the voice of God in my life?

2. In what moments of my life have I clearly felt that God has spoken to me?

3. What distractions might be keeping me from hearing the Spirit's guidance?

4. Am I obedient to the impressions I receive, or do I doubt and ignore them?

5. What changes can I make in my daily routine to be more in tune with God's will?

Steps to take action:

1. Make time for silence and reflection.

Turn off the noise of the world and seek quiet moments to listen for God's voice.

2. Keep a spiritual journal.

Write down impressions you receive while praying or reading the scriptures. Over time, you'll begin to recognize patterns in how God speaks to you.

3. Pray with intention and ask specific questions.

Be clear in your prayers and stay open to the answers that may come in different ways.

4. Be obedient to the impressions you receive.

Even if you don't understand the immediate purpose, follow the guidance God places in your heart.

5. Strengthen your relationship with God through study and worship.

Read the scriptures, attend church, and surround yourself with people who strengthen your faith.

CHAPTER 4

GOD'S TIMING

*"Todo tiene su tiempo, y todo lo que se
quiere debajo del cielo tiene su hora."*
- Eclesiastés 3:1

We live in an age of immediacy. With just one click, we can
shop, watch videos, or learn something new. This speed
has made us lose a bit of awareness about time and has taken away
our patience, since it's now so easy to get almost anything instantly.

For example, people used to grow and wait for seasonal fruits,
but nowadays, with nearby supermarkets and online stores, we can
get whatever we want at any time. In my case, I don't even need
to go to the store anymore; I shop online, choose the delivery
time, and everything arrives at my door. This change in speed and
convenience has also affected our values. One of those lost values
is the ability to wait.

These days, children don't know how to wait, and as parents,
we often give them what they want right away to avoid the crying,

teaching them to expect instant gratification. But developing patience is essential in life.

This need for immediacy affects not only our daily expectations but also how we expect results in everything: we want to lose weight fast, build muscle instantly, learn an instrument without effort, or master a skill in just a few days. But in reality, nothing of real value works that way. Everything meaningful takes time, effort, and dedication.

What's truly worthwhile takes time, has an order, and fulfills its purpose best when that time is respected.

It's in the process—in the practice, in the perseverance, and in the consistency—that we develop skills, strengthen our character, and learn to appreciate achievements.

I've also fallen into impatience. I've wanted things to happen quickly. But through Moroni's journey, I've learned that everything happens in a different time—even if that lesson came with pain and many difficult experiences. I've already told you about Moroni's feeding challenges.

From a very young age, he underwent several swallow studies, where doctors told us he had oral dysphagia—meaning he had trouble moving food from his mouth to his throat. On top of that, he suffered from aspiration: water was entering his lungs.

Because of that, he received a therapy called VitalStim, where electrodes were placed on his throat and electrical impulses were applied. Each session lasted at least 45 minutes, and the goal was for him to tolerate stronger impulses. The therapy aimed to strengthen his throat muscles, but for it to really work, Moroni had to be chewing and eating during the session. Since he couldn't do that properly, the benefits were limited.

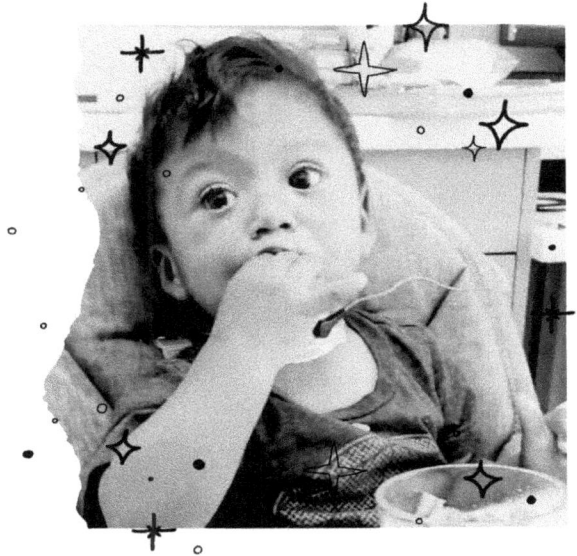

After many failed attempts with various therapies, his therapist determined he needed something more intensive. A referral was made for Moroni to be admitted to the hospital for a month of intensive feeding therapy. It wasn't a surgery or invasive procedure—he would just be under constant supervision and receive therapy at every meal, unlike his regular sessions which only happened twice a week. Intensive therapy would give him access to therapists throughout the day and greatly improve his chances of progress.

Moroni was about three years old and didn't know how to chew properly—he couldn't grind food with his molars. Learning to chew was a medical necessity for him. His inability to do so affected his entire nutrition and increased his risk of aspiration. That's why this intensive therapy was so essential.

I completed all the necessary paperwork and waited for a date. It was an exhausting process with constant phone calls to check for cancellations and open slots. I insisted, I pushed, I called therapists who had access to help speed up the process, and I spoke to those in charge to make sure my son got a spot. Due to the lack of beds in hospitals, availability was very limited, but finally, we were given a date. I felt so happy, thinking the dream of my son improving his eating would finally come true. I had knocked on not one, but many doors so he could be admitted to the hospital. I had done my part—everything in my power.

But just days before the scheduled date, I received a phone call informing me that the appointment was canceled because the insurance wouldn't cover the costs. I was stunned. I called to confirm, and sure enough, the insurance had denied the request, arguing that it wasn't necessary and that Moroni could continue with his regular therapy sessions.

I felt desperate. The hospital staff handling the insurance tried making calls to appeal the decision, and I decided to appeal on my own as well. I wrote a letter and included references and letters from multiple specialists explaining the urgency of the therapy. It was a long and frustrating process, and every time the answer was the same: the insurance company didn't see the intensive therapy as necessary. In the end, we achieved nothing—not me, and not even the hospital.

I remember how deeply that frustration and helplessness affected me. I began to feel things I had never experienced before. I had a burning sensation in my chest that wouldn't go away—an anger that consumed me—because I had invested so much time in calls, research, and solutions, only to feel like all that effort was in vain. My son truly needed this help, and I felt completely powerless.

It was at this moment that my friend, the psychologist Nora Elicema, helped me see something I hadn't considered before. Sometimes, when things don't go as we hoped, we tend to blame God or think everything happens because **"God wanted it that way."** But Nora explained to me that, although God certainly wants the best for us, He doesn't force anyone to act a certain way. He gave us free will to make our own choices, and many of the injustices we face are the result of human decisions. The insurance company's refusal to cover Moroni's therapy wasn't God's will—it was the outcome of a flawed system and of people who didn't see how urgent his case was.

She also pointed out something very wise: we often store our emotions deep inside our hearts without expressing them, and that can lead to anxiety, stress, or even physical pain. She recommended something very special—she told me to ask my husband to take the kids out for a while so I could be alone at home. She suggested I scream with all my strength, that I let it all out, even if I didn't have the words—even if only groans came out. That release would help my body process everything I was feeling and allow me to let go of all that built-up frustration.

I followed her advice. I locked myself in the house, took a deep breath... and screamed. I screamed with all my strength, letting out the powerlessness, the anger, the sadness, the exhaustion. I screamed for my son, for his pain, for the injustice of not being able to receive the help he so desperately needed.

It was, without a doubt, an unfair situation. Moroni needed more than I could offer at home, and the system had slammed the door in his face. But in the middle of that emotional storm, I realized a great truth: life is full of injustices, and if we don't learn to let them go, they stay inside and slowly destroy us.

After crying, screaming, and feeling completely broken, I decided to let go of what I couldn't control. I accepted that, for some reason, that therapy wasn't meant for Moroni. I understood that in this life, we sometimes suffer because of other people's decisions, but that doesn't mean we have to stay stuck in the pain. We can find our way toward new opportunities. As the saying goes, **"When one door closes, another one opens."** And it's true. God showed me that, in His time, all injustices can turn into something good.

That didn't mean I stopped trying. Giving up was never an option. Every single day, I modeled how to chew. During every meal, I exaggerated the motion of opening and closing my mouth, like a game. **"Nom, nom, nom"** I'd say, showing him with my mouth and hands how to do it. Sometimes I felt like a crazy woman, especially when we went out to eat as a family and we were all doing the same thing—opening and closing our mouths so he could watch us. I'm sure some people looked at us funny, but to us, it was an act of love and faith.

"It does not matter how slowly you go as long as you do not stop."

- Confucius

We kept offering different foods, even though most attempts didn't work. But I kept trying. Just to give you an idea of how weak Moroni's oral muscles were: he couldn't even chew small pieces of watermelon. Ever since he was a baby, instead of chewing, he would dissolve food using his tongue and palate, making a forward-and-back motion.

Psalm 27:14

He also coughed constantly and often choked, as if he couldn't breathe. It wasn't from food—it was that his swallowing wasn't well coordinated with his breathing, which caused these choking episodes. Eventually, we got used to seeing it at home as part of our routine, but deep down, it always hurt. However, when my mom or others saw him in that state, they would get scared and yell at us to help him. We would calmly respond, **"He's okay."**

Ironically, he wasn't okay. We didn't rush to help or do anything because, sadly, that was his daily condition. Even though it shouldn't have been normal, it was for him. And, heartbreakingly, there wasn't much more we could do beyond what we were already doing.

And so, time passed. I never stopped working with him; my love for Moroni drove me to give it my all. Maybe he didn't have therapists available like those in the intensive feeding program, but he had a mom who wouldn't give up.

The following year, Moroni gave us an incredible surprise. One day, he picked up an apple and started chewing it. Tears of joy streamed down my face. Chewing an apple was something that had once seemed impossible.

Today, my son eats chicken, beef, tacos, tostadas, and many other foods that he's learned to enjoy at four years old. It took several years for him to develop the ability to chew and move his tongue and jaw correctly.

Recently, my kids and I were sitting at the table when Abby asked me for some grapes. I brought them out and placed them on a plate. Abby began eating them, and suddenly, Moroni reached out his little hand and grabbed one. We thought he'd probably just throw it or play with it, as he usually did. But to our surprise, Moroni put the grape in his mouth and started chewing it. Abby looked at me with wide eyes and exclaimed, **"Look, Mom!"** We were both in disbelief. Moroni finished that grape, grabbed another, and then another—until he had eaten several. It was a moment of wonder and happiness we'll never forget.

This has taught me that it's essential to allow things to happen in their own time and to let the process unfold naturally. It's important to trust that God is working in our lives, even if sometimes it seems slow. Moroni learned in his own time; we didn't change anything drastically. We kept the same routine, modeling for him daily, challenging him and encouraging him. Even though he didn't respond the way we hoped at the time, eventually he understood and began to imitate the way we chewed.

In one of Moroni's last swallow studies, he still showed signs of aspiration, even after surgery and all the VitalStim therapies. I asked the feeding therapist conducting the study, **"If Moroni has aspiration, how come he hasn't had any lung infections?"** She responded, **"I don't know—Moroni is very strong."**

Then I asked again, **"If water gets into the lungs, is there a risk of infection?"** and she said yes. And yet, Moroni has never had a lung infection, despite the risk of aspiration. This is just one more proof that even when we don't receive exactly what we ask and hope for, God still performs other miracles to bless us.

I've also learned how to stay calm in difficult moments, to trust the process, and to strengthen my faith. I've developed better communication skills and learned to find creative solutions to challenges. I now know how to manage my emotions during times of frustration, and how to support my children through theirs.

These emotional and spiritual strengths I've gained, I now apply to raising my other children. I used to be less patient with them, but now I'm able to teach them how to face their own struggles with love, perseverance, and gratitude.

These experiences have given me a new perspective full of compassion. I've discovered that there are always more ways to face and solve problems than we can imagine. And if we have God on our side, we can be sure that we will be victorious in every moment.

The most valuable lesson I've learned is that, as children of God, we've inherited the ability to learn, persevere, and overcome any challenge.

It doesn't matter if the process takes one day or fifty years—if we are patient and work with dedication, we will receive what we truly deserve. And I'm certain it will be far more extraordinary than anything we ever imagined.

Nothing brightens Moroni's day like a big slice of watermelon.

Questions to ponder:

1. What practical steps could you take right now to align with God's will?

2. Which personal attributes could you strengthen to trust more in God's timing? (e.g., patience, faith, or gratitude)

3. When things don't go as expected, how do you react? Are you able to wait without frustration or anger? How could you improve your attitude during those seasons of waiting?

4. Can you identify times in your life when, after patiently waiting, blessings came in a better way than you expected?

5. How could you support others who are in their own waiting seasons—by sharing your testimony or offering encouragement?

Steps to take action:

1. Dedicate 10 minutes each day to reading about patience in Scripture or inspirational books, reflecting on how you can apply it in your life.

2. Practice patience in a specific situation—whether it's waiting in line, dealing with traffic, or resolving a conflict. Notice your reactions and work on improving each day.

3. Surround yourself with people or resources that inspire you to keep a positive perspective and trust in God's perfect timing.

4. Pray specifically for the strength and peace to wait on God's timing with faith and hope.

5. Take time when needed to reflect on your emotions and express them honestly. Talk with your family or trusted friends about how you feel during seasons of waiting. Sharing your thoughts not only strengthens your relationships but also brings emotional support and spiritual clarity.

CHAPTER 5

EFFORT AS PART OF GOD'S PLAN

"No discipline seems pleasant at the time, but
painful. Later on, however, it produces a har-
vest of righteousness and peace for those who
have been trained by it."

- Hebrews 12:11

From the beginning, God taught us that effort would be a fundamental part of our lives. In Genesis 3:19, after Adam and Eve were cast out of the Garden of Eden, the Lord said, **"By the sweat of your brow you will eat your food until you return to the ground."**

This scripture teaches us that God designed the plan so we could learn, grow, and be strengthened through work and perseverance. This principle still applies to our lives today. Nothing truly worthwhile comes without effort.

God could have allowed Adam and Eve to continue living in comfort in the Garden of Eden, but His plan was much greater. He wanted them—and us—to learn for ourselves how to discern right from wrong, to overcome challenges, to appreciate the fruit of our labors, to gain knowledge, and to trust Him every step of the way.

In order to gain knowledge, complete meaningful work, and overcome our trials, we must pay a price. That price may include sacrifice, time, energy, physical and emotional effort, stepping out of our comfort zone, self-discipline, and patience.

We often wish everything could be easy, but we forget that the most valuable blessings come when we are willing to work hard. It is in that effort that we are truly transformed, overcome obstacles, and learn to treasure what we have achieved.

The sweat of our brow is not a punishment; it is an opportunity to show ourselves that we are capable of great things through dedication. At the same time, it is a way to show our faith and gratitude.

Hebreos 12:6
"Porque el Señor disciplina al que ama, y azota a todo el que recibe por hijo"

The Lesson of the Gardener and the Currant Bush

This reminds me of a very special video titled The Will of God, presented by Elder Todd Christofferson. You can find this video on YouTube or on the official website of The Church of Jesus Christ of Latter-day Saints: https://www.churchofjesuschrist. org/media/video/2012-01-0014-the-will-of-god?lang=eng

This video uses a beautiful analogy to teach us about the purpose behind the trials and challenges we face in life. I highly recommend you look it up and watch it.

In the video, a story is told about a gardener who was tending to his garden and noticed that a currant bush was not producing fruit. He decided to prune it. As he cut the branches, he saw small drops come out—almost like tears—and imagined the currant bush saying, **"How could you do this to me? Why are you hurting me?"**

The gardener responded with patience and love: **"I am the gardener here. I know what you are meant to become, and I don't want you to be just a shade bush. I want you to bear fruit. I want you to reach your full potential."**

Over time, the currant bush blossomed, grew, and produced abundant fruit. This simple story holds a powerful message. Just as the gardener prunes and cares for the currant bush so it can grow strong and fruitful, our Heavenly Father also prunes us throughout our lives.

Sometimes those **"prunings"** come in the form of opposition, trials, challenges, loss, or injustices that hurt. They take away things we thought we needed, push us out of our comfort zones, or demand more than we think we can handle.

It's natural to ask, **"Why is this happening to me? Why does it hurt so much?"**

But we must remember that God is the Master Gardener. He sees our potential—not only who we are now, but who we can become. He doesn't want us to remain **"shade bushes"**; He wants us to bear good fruit, to reach our highest potential as sons and daughters of God.

The commandment to **"Be ye therefore perfect, even as your Father which is in heaven is perfect"** (Matthew 5:48) reminds us that we are called to grow and develop—to gain knowledge, wisdom, and virtues that reflect His divinity. And many times, these prunings are necessary to remove what holds us back and to help us discover inner strength, try new things, reshape our character, and accomplish all that we are meant to do.

This video has been a comfort to me in difficult times. When I've felt overwhelmed by trials, I watch it, and it reminds me that everything has a purpose—even pain.

Just as the currant bush was pruned to bear fruit, so are we. God, in His infinite love, allows trials to shape us—not to hurt us, but to prepare us for something better. In the end, those prunings bring us closer to Him, make us stronger, and allow us to reflect His love and purpose in our lives.

If everything in life were easy, if we received everything we wanted without effort—what would we learn? What kind of character would we develop? How would we grow?

Whenever we face a challenge and put in the effort—whether it's learning a new skill, becoming better at our work, or improving as people in our relationships or at home—that daily effort transforms us. The process of searching, struggling, falling, and rising again shapes us. Yes, we get tired, but with each step, we develop inner strength, perseverance, and the ability to face challenges with optimism.

This is clearly seen in sports. Athletes sweat, get tired, and surely have moments when they want to give up. They have bad days and good days, but when they reach the goal they've been striving for, they know it was all worth it. That feeling of satisfaction is the result of their effort and dedication—and the same applies to our daily lives and the challenges we face.

In the end, this process strengthens our self-esteem. We realize we are capable of much more than we imagined, and that increases our sense of worth and purpose. It also boosts our confidence, lifts our spirits, and helps us become better learners. God created us with the potential to be strong and resilient—and that potential only develops when we face opposition and overcome it through effort and patience.

As Romans 5:3–4 says: **"Not only so, but we also glory in tribulations, knowing that tribulation produces perseverance; perseverance, character; and character, hope."** This passage reminds us that every step in the process of making an effort is a blessing, because it builds eternal qualities within us.

What we gain easily may seem less valuable, but what we achieve through sacrifice and dedication becomes a source of lasting joy and satisfaction.

God's path is straight and narrow—not so we can look for shortcuts, but so we can walk it with faith and determination, trusting that we will reach the final destination successfully.

Within our daily effort lies the secret of our true strength and our connection to Him.

There's a story in the Bible that many of you may already know: the story of Joseph, who was sold into Egypt. Joseph had older brothers who felt great envy, anger, and resentment toward him because he was loved by their father, who had made him a special coat. In Genesis 37:3–4 we read:

"Now Israel loved Joseph more than all his children, because he was the son of his old age; and he made him a tunic of many colors. But when his brothers saw that their father loved him more than all his brothers, they hated him and could not speak peaceably to him."

Blinded by envy, his brothers decided to sell him as a slave. At first, they planned to kill him, but they eventually sold him to Ishmaelite traders who were on their way to Egypt. They deceived their father by taking Joseph's tunic, staining it with blood, and making him believe a wild animal had devoured him. Genesis 37:28 says:

"Then there passed by Midianites merchantmen; and they drew and lifted up Joseph out of the pit, and sold Joseph to the Ishmeelites for twenty pieces of silver: and they brought Joseph into Egypt."

Joseph, betrayed and heartbroken, arrived in Egypt where he was sold to Potiphar, an officer of Pharaoh. But Joseph kept a positive attitude and his faith in God. Genesis 39:2–3 says:

"The Lord was with Joseph, and he was a successful man; and he was in the house of his master the Egyptian.

And his master saw that the Lord was with him and that the Lord made all he did to prosper in his hand."

Because of his faithfulness and hard work, Potiphar made him overseer of his house, and everything Potiphar owned prospered because of Joseph. But Potiphar's wife cast her eyes on him and desired to lie with him. Joseph, being faithful to God, refused. In Genesis 39:9 we read his response: **"How then can I do this great wickedness, and sin against God?"**

Angered by the rejection, Potiphar's wife falsely accused him of trying to dishonor her. Believing his wife, Potiphar had Joseph thrown in prison. Joseph had acted justly, but still faced another injustice. While in prison, he likely felt sadness, anguish, and discouragement. He could have asked, **"Why is this happening to me if I've been faithful to God and done what's right?"**

Even though Joseph was human and surely felt pain and frustration, he did not let those feelings consume him. Instead of focusing on his circumstances, he trusted God and continued to act with integrity. Genesis 39:21 says: **"But the Lord was with Joseph and showed him mercy, and He gave him favor in the sight of the keeper of the prison."**

Even in prison, Joseph stood out. He was placed in charge of other prisoners and continued to demonstrate his faith and trust in God. He interpreted the dreams of two of Pharaoh's servants—the cupbearer and the baker—predicting accurately what would happen to them. In Genesis 40:8 Joseph says:

"Do not interpretations belong to God? Tell them to me, please."

Though he wished to be released and was innocent, Joseph waited patiently for God's timing. His faith not only sustained him, but also strengthened his character and trust in the divine plan.

Years passed until Pharaoh had a dream that no one could interpret. Then, the cupbearer remembered Joseph and told Pharaoh about him. In Genesis 41:14–15, Joseph is summoned:

Then Pharaoh sent and called Joseph, and they brought him quickly out of the dungeon; and he shaved, changed his clothing, and came to Pharaoh. And Pharaoh said to Joseph, **"I have had a dream, and there is no one who can interpret it. But I have heard it said of you that you can understand a dream, to interpret it."**

Joseph explained that Egypt would face seven years of abundance followed by seven years of famine. He gave Pharaoh a plan to store food during the years of plenty. In Genesis 41:38–39, Pharaoh recognizes Joseph's wisdom:

"Can we find such a one as this, a man in whom is the Spirit of God? Then Pharaoh said to Joseph, 'Inasmuch as God has shown you all this, there is no one as discerning and wise as you.'"

Pharaoh appointed Joseph as governor of Egypt. When the famine came, Joseph's brothers traveled to Egypt after hearing that there was food there. Joseph recognized them, but they did not recognize him. In Genesis 45:4–5, Joseph reveals himself and forgives them:

"I am Joseph your brother, whom you sold into Egypt. But now, do not therefore be grieved or angry with yourselves

because you sold me here; for God sent me before you to preserve life."

Joseph brought his family—including his father Jacob—to Egypt, where they lived in the land of Goshen.

Thanks to his faith, perseverance, and loyalty, Joseph not only saved his family, but an entire nation. Genesis 50:20 sums up his perspective:

"You intended to harm me, but God intended it for good, to accomplish what is now being done, the saving of many lives."

Remember when we spoke about injustice in the previous chapter?

Life is full of injustices. Do you know why? Because God gave us all the ability to choose between good and evil.

God wants us to choose the good, because He knows it brings us power, protection, and blessings. However, in this life, we must live by faith, because we can't remember His plan or see it with our earthly eyes.

God cannot force others to do what is right, to treat us fairly, or to give us what we need and deserve. But He is always there to guide us and give us strength through our trials.

The story of Joseph in Egypt is one of my favorites, and I consider him one of the heroes I admire most. His life teaches us valuable lessons about hope, humility, charity, forgiveness, responsibility, perseverance, dedication, commitment, and love.

In the same way, if you are facing difficult trials in your life—especially those caused by others—remember this promise:

God can turn even the most painful experiences into blessings if you trust in Him and keep trying every day.

Questions to ponder:

1. Have I ever been in difficult situations where injustice affected me emotionally? How did I handle those situations, and what did I learn from them?

2. When things get tough, do I tend to complain or give up? Or do I see them as opportunities to push myself and seek new tools?

3. In what ways can I strengthen my ability to choose what is right, even when facing challenges or temptations?

4. What concrete steps can I take to transform injustice or hardship into opportunities for personal and spiritual growth?

Steps to take action:

1. When you face a challenge, take a moment to identify how you can turn that difficulty into an opportunity. Think about new tools or creative ways to approach it.

2. Choose a person or situation that has caused you pain and, even if it's hard, pray for that person and search your heart for a way to practice forgiveness.

3. Plan something tangible that shows effort and perseverance—a personal project, a habit you want to change, or a goal you want to achieve.

4. Surround yourself with people or resources that inspire you to keep a positive perspective and to trust in God's perfect timing.

5. Practice perseverance every day. You don't have to do everything perfectly—just be consistent. Take small steps forward, no matter how insignificant they may seem. Fulfill your daily responsibilities, but make a conscious effort to do them with a joyful heart and a positive attitude. By doing this, you train your mind and spirit to face challenges with greater strength and optimism.

CHAPTER 6

MINISTRATION OF ANGELS

"Then an angel from heaven appeared to
him and strengthened him."

- Luke 22:43

One of the most sacred moments found in the Bible is when Jesus Christ, the beloved Son of God, offered Himself to pay for our sins. In that moment of solitude and agony, in the Garden of Gethsemane, He knelt and prayed, saying:

"Father, if you are willing, take this cup from me; yet not my will, but yours be done" (Luke 22:42).

His prayer reflects perfect submission to the will of the Father, even in the midst of unimaginable suffering.

The Firstborn of the Father was experiencing indescribable pain. No parent wants to see their child suffer, and our Heavenly Father, being all-powerful, witnessed this infinite act of love without stepping in to take the pain away.

However, in His perfect love, He sent an angel to strengthen His beloved Son.

Jesus—blameless, sinless, and perfect like His Father—suffered what He did not deserve. He did it out of love for us, to give us the opportunity to be clean and worthy to return to our Heavenly Father. As Isaiah 53:5 declares:

"But he was wounded for our transgressions, he was bruised for our iniquities; the chastisement of our peace was upon him, and by his stripes we are healed."

This story touches me deeply because Jesus Christ, in His divinity and perfection, received comfort and support from an angel. His example teaches us that even He, with His infinite power, needed help during such a difficult moment. This reminds us that we are not alone in our trials; Heavenly Father will also send comfort and strength when we need it most.

Throughout my life, I've heard many stories of angelic intervention. There are even books and movies that share how people have experienced divine help in critical moments. I firmly believe in the existence of angels and that God sends them daily to strengthen us.

It's important to understand that not all angels come from heaven or from the other side of the veil. There are also angels who live here on earth—who walk beside us, live in our neighborhoods, and share our everyday lives. These people, filled with charity, bring heaven closer to us and become earthly angels who, like heavenly ones, bless our lives.

The true story behind the film The Cokeville Miracle took place in 1986 in the town of Cokeville, Wyoming. A man and his wife brought a bomb to an elementary school intending to take the lives of the children and staff.

Besides its explosive capacity, the bomb contained nails that would act as deadly projectiles upon detonation.

That day, many of the children, being believers, prayed for protection. When the bomb exploded, incredibly, no one was harmed.

In the days that followed, some children reported having seen angels who called them by name and helped them escape. When shown photos of deceased relatives, they identified those angels as their own grandparents, great-grandparents, or family members.

They also described flashes of light that shielded them from the fire. If you're interested in learning more about this event, I encourage you to watch the movie.

Our Heavenly Father knows our burdens and our struggles, and when we need it most, He sends reinforcements—whether through visible angels or ordinary people acting as His hands here on earth.

A Testimony of Divine Love

In this book, I share many stories from our life with Moroni. As I've mentioned before, his condition has led him to face numerous physical challenges, which have meant countless hospital visits and sleepless nights. One of those nights helped me see that God's love is real—and that He always cares for us.

It all began when I noticed that Moroni had blood in his diaper. Although I knew it was something that needed to be addressed immediately, I resisted the idea of taking him to the hospital yet again.

My body, my mind, my eyes—everything was at its limit. The constant sleep deprivation and the emotional and physical toll had pushed me to the edge of exhaustion. And I knew I was in for another long and uncomfortable night.

I waited for my husband to get home from work so he could stay with Abby and Mahonri, and then I took Moroni to the hospital. As expected, we spent hours waiting for Moroni to be seen. They also had to draw blood multiple times, poking him in different spots because his veins were so small that the procedure was difficult. They tried several times before succeeding. Moroni cried a lot—being moved from one test to another only made him more upset.

Finally, around four in the morning, we were admitted to a small hospital room. They told us they would wait a few hours before doing more detailed tests to rule out intestinal complications and to find out why his liver enzymes were alarmingly high.

The room was small, with a tall crib and a sleeper chair beside it. I was so exhausted that the moment I lay down, I fell into a deep sleep.

As usual, Moroni started crying not long after.

My body wouldn't move, even though my mind was aware that he was crying. I heard the nurse gently soothing him, patting his chest or back and whispering **"shh, shh, shh"** to calm him down.

In my mind, I felt deeply grateful for the kindness of that nurse who took the time to comfort my son. Moroni settled down, but after a while, he began crying again.

"Behold, I send an Angel before thee, to keep thee in the way, and to bring thee into the place which I have prepared".

EXODUS 23:20

Once again, I heard the same lullabies, the same gentle pats, and even the squeaking of the crib as it moved—just like when my husband or I would soothe him at home.

Even though I was completely exhausted, in my mind I kept thinking the nurse must be judging me—thinking I was a bad mother for not getting up. But I was so depleted that even though I wanted to care for my baby, I physically couldn't.

When Moroni cried for the third time, and I once again heard the same soothing **"shh, shh, shh,"** I decided that it was enough—I had to get up.

Gathering all the strength I had left, I said, **"I'm coming."** As I stood up with determination to comfort him myself, I realized there was no nurse in the room.

I was confused—maybe she was crouched next to the crib? I looked under it, but no one was there. I assumed she had left the room, so I peeked into the hallway and found a long, empty corridor. Not a soul in sight.

Another flash of light. Suddenly, a strange and powerful feeling came over me—and I understood something: it hadn't been a nurse. Moroni wasn't in the intensive care unit, so there wasn't a nurse assigned solely to him. And there were no cameras or monitors keeping a constant watch on him.

In that moment, I knew with certainty that it had been an angel sent by God—to comfort Moroni and to let me rest.

That thought filled me with overwhelming gratitude.

I felt how deeply my Heavenly Father loved me—so much that He sent an angel to care for my child and to give me the rest I so desperately needed.

As I reflected on that experience, a strong impression came to my heart—so clear, so sweet—that revealed to me that the angel was my sister-in-law Lorena, who had passed away from cancer.

I felt that God had allowed her to come help us—me and Moroni—at a moment of extreme need. That experience was so tender, so full of love, that I will never forget it.

The heavens opened for me that night, and I felt with absolute certainty that God will always be there for me.

His love is infinite. It doesn't matter what situation we're in—if it's important to us, it is important to our Heavenly Father. There is no situation too small for Him.

Others may think it's insignificant, but to our Creator, it is just as meaningful and precious.

The Room Where an Angel Came to Visit Us.

I want to share another very special experience. All the stories I share in this book are not in chronological order, so I'm going back to the time when Moroni had open-heart surgery.

I've already shared part of this event, but I want to return to a detail that relates to the topic of divine help.

That surgery was one of the longest and most difficult we've ever faced. My husband and I decided not to leave the hospital, since we could be called at any moment with news about our son. To pass the time, we started walking through the hospital hallways.

On the first floor, there is a small multi-faith chapel—a place of prayer with various holy scriptures and benches to sit or kneel. I had walked past that place many times before, since it's on the way to the cafeteria, but I always found it empty. In fact, I only remember seeing someone there once. But this time was different.

We entered the chapel to pray. We picked up a Bible and began reading and pleading with God to take care of Moroni—that He would allow us to have him with us for many more years.

As we sat there, a dark-skinned man walked in, dressed in nurse's scrubs and wearing a hospital badge. He stood in front of us, clearly determined to deliver a message. His demeanor was kind and welcoming.

He began to speak to us and, without hesitation, took the Bible and started reading us several scriptures. I don't remember exactly which verses he read or the specific words he said, but what I do remember was the kindness in his voice, the deep knowledge he had of God's Word, and his sincere desire to comfort us through the scriptures.

His words were so full of comfort and faith that they filled our hearts with hope and peace. We could feel the Spirit of God touching our souls through the words of this man.

After a while, he left. As my husband and I stepped out of the chapel, we began to talk about what had just happened. We were surprised that someone had approached us in such a comforting way—especially someone we didn't know.

2 Kings 6:15–17

15 And when the servant of the man of God was risen early, and gone forth, behold, an host compassed the city both with horses and chariots. And his servant said unto him, Alas, my master! how shall we do?

16 And he answered, Fear not: for they that be with us are more than they that be with them.

17 And Elisha prayed, and said, Lord, I pray thee, open his eyes, that he may see. And the Lord opened the eyes of the young man; and he saw: and, behold, the mountain was full of horses and chariots of fire round about Elisha.

Reflecting on the experience, we came to the conclusion that perhaps he wasn't just an ordinary person. Maybe he was an angel.

I can't say with certainty whether he was a heavenly angel, but I am sure he was an angel—whether earthly or divine—because he brought comfort and hope to our souls in a critical moment.

All of these experiences, the stories from the Bible, and the testimonies I've heard from others fill my heart with hope.

Now that the years have passed and I continue facing health challenges with my older children, these experiences have given me strength and help me feel confident that, in the end, everything will be okay.

I have no reason to doubt, because my Heavenly Father has given me too many signs that His love is great and that He will never let go of me.

That's why I've written this book: I want to show you—yes, you who are reading these pages—that God is also your Heavenly Father. Just as He created me, He created you; just as He thinks of me, He thinks of you; and just as He has sent angels to help me, He sends them to you too.

Don't be afraid. Don't give up. Believe and trust.

Place your life in His hands, and you will begin to see life through heavenly eyes. Everything will start to make more sense, and with spiritual eyes, you will begin to understand that everything has a divine purpose.

You will overcome whatever you are facing day by day.

God loves you. He will care for you. And He will strengthen you.

"At times, either as individuals or as groups, we may feel that we are far from God, cast out of heaven, lost and alone in dark and dreary places.
Often that distress is of our own making, but even then, the Father of us all is watching and assisting.
And always there are angels who come and go around us, seen and unseen, known and unknown, mortal and immortal."

- Jeffrey R. Holland

Questions to ponder:

1.   Have you ever felt the presence of someone very special in your life who filled you with peace, comfort, and hope?

2.   Can you remember a moment when you felt that God sent someone at exactly the right time, just when you needed it most?

3.   How has the selfless service of others impacted your life?

4.   Have you ever felt prompted or inspired to help someone, and later realized it was exactly what they needed?

5.   How could you be more aware of the opportunities to be an angel for someone else?

6.   What stories—from your own life or from others—have strengthened your testimony that angels are among us?

7.   Have you ever felt an unexplainable peace during a trial, as if you were being supported by a heavenly presence?

Steps to take action:

1. Recognize the angels in your life.

Reflect on the people who have been a blessing along your journey and find a special way to thank them.

2. Be an angel for someone else.

Do a spontaneous act of kindness—whether by offering help, sharing a word of encouragement, or simply listening to someone who needs it.

3. Pay attention to the promptings of the Holy Spirit.

Many times, God inspires us to help someone at the exact moment they need it. Learn to recognize those promptings and act quickly.

4. Learn about the ministration of angels in the Scriptures.

Discover how God has sent angels to help His people in the past—and how He continues to do so today.

5. Share your testimony of earthly angels.

If you've felt divine help through someone, share it. Your story might strengthen someone else's faith.

CHAPTER 7

THE GIFTS OF GOD

"Each of you should use whatever gift
you have received to serve others, as
faithful stewards of God's grace in its
various forms."

- 1 Peter 4:10

Our Heavenly Father, the Creator of the universe and of our bodies, is a supreme, all-powerful, all-knowing, and ever-present Being. He knows everything, sees everything, and His wisdom is infinite. It is impossible for us to fully comprehend His majesty and glory, for His power and light are beyond our human understanding.

As His children, we have inherited many of His divine qualities, virtues, and intelligence. It is beautiful to reflect on how He has shared with us a portion of His gifts, talents, and abilities.

These gifts are a manifestation of His infinite love for us and a tool to help us fulfill our purpose here on earth.

Our world is incredibly beautiful because of the diversity within it. We are all different—and those differences make us perfect in God's eyes. Each of us has been blessed with unique talents that enrich not only our own lives but also the lives of others. Our existence is elevated not only by the gifts we possess but by those that others share with us as well.

I'd like to share a story from the Bible that many of you may already know, and if not, I'm sure you'll love it. It's one of the parables—stories Jesus used to teach powerful lessons—and it's called **The Parable of the Talents**, found in Matthew 25:14–30.

A man went on a journey and entrusted his servants with his belongings:

* **To one he gave five talents,**
* **To another, two talents,**
* **And to another, one talent—each according to their ability.**

A "talent" in this context was a large amount of money.

1. The servant who received five talents worked with them and earned five more.

2. The one who received two talents also traded and gained two more.

3. But the one who received a single talent, out of fear, buried it and did nothing with it.

When the master returned, he called each servant to account: To the first two, he said: **"Well done, good and faithful servant!"**

You were faithful with a few things; I will put you in charge of many things. Enter into the joy of your Lord."

But to the third, he said: **"You wicked, lazy servant!"** He reprimanded him for not using what he had been given and ordered that the one talent be taken from him and given to the one with ten.

God has given each of us talents, gifts, and abilities according to our individual capacity. However, many of us have not yet discovered all of them, and many we will uncover throughout our lives.

When I was pregnant with Moroni, I went through a very difficult time. I had already lost two pregnancies, and with Moroni—my third baby—the circumstances were complicated. Out of fear that something might go wrong, I was placed on strict bed rest for several months. That was a huge challenge. I've always considered myself an active woman, so being physically limited filled me with frustration.

To distract myself from those negative thoughts and emotions, I asked my husband to buy me some watercolors. I had never painted before, but I knew it was something light and easy to clean. I thought it would be a good activity while I was confined to bed. My husband bought me my first watercolors, brushes, and a special sketchbook. I started by making simple strokes—little flowers and some hand lettering. Though my drawings were rough and unpolished, I discovered that painting made me feel different. That time spent with watercolor gave me a new perspective each day. It lifted my spirits and helped me forget my worries.

Months later, Moroni was born. Life with a newborn and two other small children is demanding, and as a mother, I didn't have much time to paint. But whenever I felt overwhelmed or sad, my husband encouraged me to pick up the watercolors again while he watched the kids. Little by little, I returned to painting. I wasn't perfect—my brush strokes were still clumsy and far from professional—but the simple act of painting brought me a deep sense of calm and healing.

One day, while I was painting, I heard God speak to me—so clearly and softly at the same time. He said:

"Gabby, painting will be a tool to help you carry your burdens, because very difficult moments are coming in Moroni's life."

There have been countless times—especially during Moroni's surgeries—when this new gift from God has saved me. Many times, I brought my watercolors to the hospital. While Moroni slept, I painted, and that helped me cope with the stress and fear.

Since then, watercolor has become more than just a hobby—it has become a form of healing for my soul. It is a divine gift that has allowed me to find peace and strength during my darkest moments.

And that gift didn't just heal me—it became a source of service. When I first began painting, I practiced a lot, and we didn't have space at home to keep all the artwork. So I began giving my paintings away. Whenever I heard of someone going through a hard time, I would paint flowers for them, write inspiring quotes, or draw the hands of Jesus. On several occasions, when a friend or acquaintance lost a loved one, I created an image of Jesus standing next to that person, both dressed in white.

I know with certainty that these pieces brought hope to those who received them. And that brought me even greater joy: knowing that my talent could be shared with others, and that what I created had the power to comfort wounded hearts and bring light into painful situations.

With practice, I've improved each day. When I look back at my earliest paintings, I can see how much I've grown. I decided to enter the art contest at the Texas State Fair, and to my surprise, I won second place in the watercolor still life category in 2023. I participated again in 2024 and received an honorable mention.

I have seen with my own eyes that the promise in the Scriptures is true: God multiplies our gifts when we put them into practice. And not only that—He provides the means for us to develop those talents.

One of those means came when an older couple from Argentina started attending our church. When they introduced themselves, I learned that the husband was a professional painter, and that many of his works were displayed at the Museum of Biblical Art in Dallas, Texas. I was amazed, especially because I was just beginning to develop a serious interest in art.

Over time, we got to know Jorge and Miriam Cocco. Every Sunday, we would visit their home, which was filled with finished pieces and ongoing projects.

I was impressed not only by Jorge's amazing art, but by the humility, simplicity, and love he and his wife showed to everyone around them. I remember how Moroni would run into his studio the moment we arrived, grabbing brushes and trying to paint. I would quickly rush in to stop him from ruining any of the artwork, but Jorge always said, **"Let him paint."**

He let Moroni use his brushes however he wanted. Sometimes Moroni would get too close to completed pieces, but Jorge never got upset. A beautiful friendship grew from those moments. I would show him my rough paintings, and he would give me advice.

During one visit, Jorge told me,

"The teacher arrives when the student is ready. And you are ready."

He also told me he didn't believe it was a coincidence that we met. He was sure that God had brought our lives together, and he offered to give me lessons, teaching me different techniques. This led to many wonderful conversations about the gospel of Jesus Christ and about art.

He became a mentor to me, inspiring me to keep going and not give up. His generosity and love made me feel the love of God. It was not only that God had given me a gift—but that He was showing me the path to develop it.

I encourage you to explore his work. It's beautiful and truly unique. You can visit his website at: https://jorgecocco.com/.

Jorge Cocco Santángelo is an internationally renowned artist, famous for his **"sacrocubism"** style, which combines cubism with sacred themes. In 2021, his art was selected for a special Christmas stamp collection by the Royal Mail of the United Kingdom—a great recognition of his talent and artistic vision. His work has been exhibited in galleries and private collections around the world, and his influence continues to grow in the field of contemporary sacred art. This story is just one example of the many gifts God gives to His children.

Many people have the gift of music—a healing balm for the soul that touches hearts.

Others have the gift of singing, of filling spaces with melodies that bring peace and hope, or the talent to compose songs that inspire and connect people on a deep level.

Some have the gift of cooking with such love that their meals don't just nourish the body—they warm the hearts of those who eat them.

Others possess the ability to work with their hands, creating beauty in the world, or the gift of strength, which they use to help others—whether by lifting physical burdens or supporting someone emotionally in times of need.

Some have the gift of listening—what a wonderful gift that is. To listen with true empathy and attention is an act of love.

It allows others to feel heard, understood, and valued. It's a gift that not only heals the speaker, but also strengthens bonds between hearts. There are those who have the gift of motivation—to inspire others to rise up when they feel they can't go on.

These people are like lighthouses that illuminate the path, reminding us that there is always hope, and that we can accomplish great things when someone believes in us. They're friends, family, or even strangers whose words or actions lift us and push us to become better.

The gift of smiling and being joyful is a wonderful blessing. There are people whose energy is so contagious, whose charisma

every good gift
and every perfect
gift is from
above

James 1:17

is so natural, that they lift our spirits with their sense of humor, cheerful words, and joyful presence.

I'm especially grateful for my husband, Jorge. He listens to me with patience and love, and I deeply admire his ability to put himself in other people's shoes. He has a special gift: thinking of others' needs before his own. No matter what's going on, he always finds a way to encourage me to pursue my dreams—whether it's helping with the kids, doing housework, or stepping in wherever needed—he does it all without complaint so I can take time to paint. That gift of selfless love and service that he has inspires me. It's a reflection of pure love—the kind that is given without expecting anything in return—and reminds me how beautiful it is to have people in our lives who support us unconditionally.

Every talent has a special purpose and a unique impact. When we share our gifts with others, we not only enrich their lives, but also our own—creating deeper connections and reflecting God's love and generosity.

Maybe you're thinking that you don't have any of these gifts. I know I haven't mentioned them all—because there are many!—and I encourage you to discover them, develop them, and share them.

You will find an inexhaustible source of peace and strength. And if you still feel like you don't have many gifts, talents, or abilities, I invite you to ask God in prayer to show you the path and help you develop the talents you desire to have.

Over the years—especially in the midst of adversity and the daily challenges of life—I've realized that I've been able to grow in gifts and abilities.

Many people ask me if there's anything I don't know how to do. It makes me laugh, because of course there are things I can't do—but I also confidently say there are many things I can do.

I love to learn and try new things—especially when they benefit my family and those around me. I do it with enthusiasm and perseverance.

God gave us these gifts for our happiness—but there is a warning: If we bury them, if we don't use them, and if we don't share them, God may take them from us—and we'll lose that channel of joy.

In a European city during World War II, a statue of Jesus Christ was severely damaged. After the war ended, the citizens decided to restore it. They were able to reconstruct almost all of it, but the hands were so shattered that they couldn't be repaired.

Instead of replacing them, the people chose to leave the statue without hands, and they placed a plaque at its base that read:

"We are His hands."

That detail symbolizes a powerful truth:

As followers of Christ, we are called to be His hands on earth—helping others and continuing His work.

Gifts are heavenly treasures that we should open with joy and gratitude. When we receive them, we must embrace them and keep in mind the love with which they were given. These gifts are not only for our benefit, but also to bless and enrich the lives of others.

Use them with purpose—and share their light!

1 Corinthians 12:4–11

"There are different kinds of gifts, but the same Spirit distributes them.
There are different kinds of service, but the same Lord.
There are different kinds of working,
but in all of them and in everyone it is the same God at work.
Now to each one the manifestation of the Spirit is given
for the common good.
To one there is given through the Spirit a message of wisdom,
to another a message of knowledge by means of the same Spirit,
to another faith by the same Spirit,
to another gifts of healing by that one Spirit,
to another miraculous powers,
to another prophecy,
to another distinguishing between spirits,
to another speaking in different kinds of tongues,
and to still another the interpretation of tongues.
All these are the work of one and the same Spirit, and he distributes them
to each one, just as he determines."

Questions to ponder:

1. Can you identify the gifts you have received from God?

2. Are you using your gifts and talents for your benefit and to bless others?

3. How has gaining new skills transformed your life?

4. Do you believe that with effort and dedication you can continue developing even more talents and abilities?

Steps to take action:

1. If you don't yet know what your gifts or talents are, take time for introspection.

Ask yourself which activities you enjoy and come naturally to you—these are often clues to your talents.

2. Pray to Heavenly Father, asking Him to guide you and help you identify the gifts He has given you.

3. If you've already identified your talents, make a list of concrete actions you can take to improve them.

Remember that when you share and give from your talents, you will receive even more.

4. Talk to friends, mentors, or family members and ask what virtues or abilities they see in you.

Once you identify them, dedicate more time and effort to developing those skills.

5. Look for opportunities to use your talents in service to others.

By doing so, you will not only bless others but also find greater purpose and fulfillment in your own life.

CHAPTER 8

GRATITUDE

"Always giving thanks to God the Father
for everything, in the name of our Lord
Jesus Christ."

- Ephesians 5:20

I want to begin this chapter with a very well-known analogy, one that has much to teach us. I'm sure you've heard it before—the glass of water analogy.

You'll find it illustrated on the next page, and I invite you to reflect on this question:

How do you see the glass of water? Do you see it as half full, or do you see it as half empty?

Some people see it as half empty, while others see it as half full.

There is no "correct" answer—it all depends on what you choose to perceive.

The way we respond to challenges and adversity in our lives greatly depends on how we decide to interpret them. It all comes down to our perspective. You can choose to focus on a life filled with gratitude and happiness, appreciating what you have—or you can let sadness and scarcity take control.

The choice is in your hands. What perspective will you choose today? Challenges may seem overwhelming, but they can also be seen as hard-earned opportunities full of growth and learning. In every situation in life, you have the power to find the light—or to remain in darkness.

The choice is always yours. Gratitude is a powerful key. It opens the door to joy, hope, and encouragement. It's easy to make long lists of what we don't have, of what's missing, or the problems we face.

In my case, I could list all the difficulties my son Moroni has faced since he was born—illnesses, surgeries, and physical limitations.

There are so many things he doesn't have that other children do enjoy. But I could also make a long list of all the things Moroni does have.

Some of his blessings include: a mom and dad who love and care for him; siblings who bring him joy and include him in activities—even ones he can't always do on his own; friends wherever he goes; and a body which, though weak and uncoordinated at times, allows him to carry out his daily activities. He can see, eat, breathe, and has a smile that fills everyone around him with tenderness and happiness.

He's also been surrounded by dedicated specialists who care deeply about his well-being, advanced therapies that have strengthened him, and loving therapists who, over the years, taught him how to move better and eat on his own. They pushed him to his limits because they believed in him—and the care and love with which they did it were priceless.

I'm grateful to each one of them for making such a difference in his life. Today, Moroni is also blessed with empathetic teachers who teach with patience, and with a school specifically for the deaf—designed for his needs and located near our area.

And why does Moroni attend a school for the deaf? Let me share that story with you. As Moroni grew, new diagnoses continued to appear, and we simply accepted them as part of what we had to face as a family.

At around five months old, Moroni was diagnosed with permanent moderate to severe hearing loss in his left ear. I remember imagining many hard scenarios my son might face as someone with hearing loss. I feared that our family wouldn't be able to communicate with him—that he would feel isolated and frustrated because he couldn't express himself. But I made a conscious decision to shift my mindset and focus on everything I had to be grateful for. After everything he had already faced since birth, this news was just another challenge.

They explained to me that it would be important for Moroni and our whole family to begin learning sign language, as it would be an essential tool for his development and future communication.

Surprisingly, instead of feeling discouraged, I felt thankful. My gratitude became a powerful force that kept me motivated and willing to learn. I thanked God for allowing us to detect the issue early, for the existence of an effective method like sign language that would help us communicate with him, and for the opportunities we still had to support his speech development—even if it would happen in a different way than most.

In August 2021, Moroni was 10 months old, and that day, he was going to receive his hearing aid. I vividly remember when the audiologist asked us, **"Are you ready to record?"**

She had everything prepared and asked me to place the device in his ear. I wish you could see his reaction—it was a gift from heaven.

If you want to experience that moment, you can search for the video on social media by typing in the search bar:

"Moroni listening to all the sounds." You'll see a baby in a stroller—and that's my Moroni.

At the end of this book, I'll include a QR code that you can scan with your phone's camera. It will take you to a link with videos of some of the moments I've shared in this book.

It's hard to describe with words what happened that day, but I'll try. When we placed the hearing aid in Moroni's ear, he was babbling. The audiologist activated the device through her computer, and in that instant, Moroni opened his eyes wide. It was clear he had heard his own voice—and he immediately began to laugh.

His reaction was so sweet because he looked genuinely surprised to hear with greater clarity. It was another moment of light. My heart was filled with gratitude, knowing that now—with the help of his device—he could hear better.

I want to add that to help him, I even learned how to sew special little hats that prevented him from pulling off the hearing aid. Sometimes he would yank it off and throw it, but the hats made it easier to keep it in place.

Every little effort was worth it.

I am also deeply grateful that we were referred to a hearing therapist who came to our home every week. She not only worked enthusiastically with Moroni—who was still very young at the time—but also focused on teaching me and my entire family. Each week, we learned new signs that became part of our daily routine.

I didn't focus on what Moroni lacked. Instead, I focused on all the blessings we were receiving: the opportunity to communicate, the technology, the specialists, and most of all—his life.

Over time, this experience filled us with motivation and joy, and we became even more committed to learning sign language. As Moroni grew, he was able to join a deaf education program, where most of his teachers use sign language.

It has been incredibly enriching to meet people with different challenges—people who have inspired us to be more inclusive and to keep improving this precious language.

Over a year ago, when Moroni was about three years old, he underwent another hearing test under sedation, since he was already scheduled for another surgery.

The doctors wanted to check whether his hearing had worsened. Since his initial diagnosis, we had been told that his hearing would gradually decline until he became completely deaf.

Although I prayed that this wouldn't happen, I also reaffirmed my commitment to God—to accept any new diagnosis Moroni might receive with faith and trust.

"Gratitude is of the very essence of worship.
… When you walk with gratitude, you do not
walk with arrogance and conceit and egotism,
you walk with a spirit of thanksgiving that is
becoming to you and will bless your lives."

- Gordon B. Hinckley

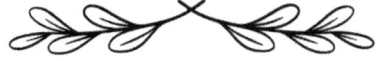

As a family, we were prepared to move forward, relying on sign language as our main tool for communication if it became necessary.

But when the audiologist came out with the results, she told me something I never expected: **"Moroni does not have hearing loss."** Surprised, I asked her, **"What are you saying?"** She confirmed, **"His hearing is normal in both ears."**

At that moment, I couldn't hold back the tears. It was an indescribable emotion, because even though I had never asked God to restore my son's hearing, He had given us this unexpected gift.

I had already accepted our situation. I was even grateful for the way it had brought our family closer and led us to learn new things.

Seeing how emotional I was, the doctor added, **"I want you to know his hearing is fluctuating. In the future, he may lose it completely. But for now, he doesn't need a hearing aid."**

That warning didn't change my joy. With or without hearing, Moroni is deeply loved, and we will always do our best to communicate with him.

Today, Moroni still hears well and no longer uses his hearing aid. This has been a miracle for our family and for all those around him. That's why gratitude is a key part of our lives. It's the foundation of our trust in God's plan and our love for Him.

I don't want this experience to be misunderstood. Being grateful doesn't mean we'll receive every miracle we hope for. I don't know why my son was granted the ability to hear again—but I am deeply grateful to have received something I never imagined would be possible.

Still, I want to make it clear that if Moroni had continued to experience hearing loss, my joy and gratitude would be the same.

We've received other blessings along the way, and those blessings are just as real and meaningful. Gratitude does not depend on the miracles we hope for—it comes from recognizing the hand of God in every detail of our lives.

The other day, I was driving home in light rain and heavy traffic. We were barely moving. My mind was full of thoughts, and I was distracted, until I realized I couldn't see clearly through the windshield.

The raindrops were blurring my vision. I couldn't keep driving safely, so I immediately turned on the windshield wipers. Within seconds, everything became clear again—the cars, the lights, the road. I could move forward with confidence.

That moment led me to reflect. I realized that when we allow feelings like pride, anger, distrust, or complaints about our circumstances to build up, it's as if each of those **"raindrops"** clouds our view.

Little by little, those feelings blur our perspective and prevent us from seeing the path clearly. In that state, fear and uncertainty take over. But if we are humble enough, we can **"turn on the wipers" of gratitude.** And in just seconds, thankfulness clears our view and allows us to recognize the wonders already present in our lives.

All we need is enough faith to activate it—and begin to see clearly again. I feel deeply grateful for my friends, acquaintances, family, and all the strangers around the world who—without even

Give Thanks in all circumstances; for this is God's will for you in Christ Jesus.

1 Thessalonians 5:18

knowing me personally—have prayed for me, for Moroni, and for my family.

I know they have, because over the years, I've received messages and comments on social media. Thousands and thousands of people have lifted up prayers—not just my followers, but also their friends, families, and coworkers.

I've even heard of entire congregations from different religions uniting in prayer for Moroni during various stages of his health journey. People have shared his story with their employers, coworkers, and loved ones. My heart overflows with joy and humility to be the recipient of so much kindness and love for my family.

If you are one of those people—thank you. Thank you from the bottom of my heart. I see God's goodness reflected in all these acts of love. Whenever we face a new diagnosis—or simply need extra help—I ask for prayers on social media, because I've seen how each one is answered.

There have been countless times when I've felt I couldn't go on, but your prayers have strengthened me and given me renewed power to continue.

Let me share a brief story.

Remember when I mentioned that Moroni spent a night in the sleep lab? Well, during that study, they had to attach more than 50 wires to his head, as well as others on his feet, hands, waist, and finally his nose—with bands near his mouth.

The nurse began attaching the wires to his head, and you can imagine the scene. Moroni began screaming and moving desperately.

Whenever I see Moroni suffer, I try to remain calm—but inside, my heart is breaking. Maybe they weren't hurting him physically, but Moroni is extremely sensitive, and he was truly overwhelmed.

The nurse said to me, **"If your son doesn't calm down, I'm going to have to tie his hands behind his back for the whole night."**

When I heard those words, I felt a mix of anger and heartbreak. I knew Moroni needed this study, and if we canceled it, it would take months to get another appointment.

I couldn't argue with her, so I simply said,

"You're not going to tie him. I'll hold him myself." It was extremely difficult to hold Moroni's body still—but I did it.

The nurse managed to attach all the wires, but the worst part came when she approached his mouth to insert the tube into his nose. Once she left the room, I burst into tears.

I wanted to scream in frustration because I saw how distressed Moroni was. But instead, I knelt down and prayed. I also sent messages to my family, asking them to pray for Moroni—to help him calm down so they wouldn't have to tie him up.

I texted several friends too. About 30 minutes later, Moroni fell asleep. And not only that—he slept through the entire night without moving. Moroni always moves a lot in his sleep—but that night, he stayed still. Completely still.

That's why I want to thank every person who has included us in their prayers. Thank you for your words, your faith, and your love toward us. God bless you!

I try to teach my children the importance of gratitude and to help them value all that God—and we as parents—give them.

I once heard a talk by Bonnie D. Parkin on gratitude, where she shared the story of a mother who decided to write down something she was thankful for every day. I thought it was a wonderful idea, so we decided to apply it in our family.

Colossians 4:2
"Devote yourselves to prayer, being watchful and thankful."

Every night before we pray and tuck them into bed, we sit together at the edge of the bed and I ask them,

"What are you grateful for today?" Each of them shares something, and I've been truly touched by their responses. At first, my son Mahonri usually wouldn't say anything. But after repeating this practice night after night, he began to mention one thing… then another… and another.

Sometimes when I try to move on to Abby, he'll stop me and say, **"Mom, I'm not finished yet,"** and continues listing more things he's grateful for.

We keep a record of everything in a little gratitude notebook, writing down each response. I even turn to Moroni and ask,

"And you, Moroni, what are you thankful for?"

Even though he can't speak, he makes sounds and little noises to show he's participating. It's a sweet and touching moment.

I hope that by the end of next year, we can pull out that notebook and read together everything we've expressed gratitude for over the months. I'm sure it will be a beautiful experience and a reminder of God's love and the blessings we've received.

For example, when the 2024–2025 school year began, my son Mahonri spent about five months saying that going to school was the worst. Every morning, he would repeat that he didn't want to go and insisted that Saturdays and Sundays were his favorite days because he didn't have to attend classes. His attitude started to worry me, so we got to work—we met with our favorite psychologist and made some changes to our routine. Then one day, just a few weeks ago, Mahonri said, **"I'm thankful I went to school."** Each of those things, no matter how small they may seem, are incredibly brave blessings for us.

I'd love to share with you a few of the things we've written in our gratitude notebook.

Some may seem simple—but to us, they are deeply meaningful:

- Because he made a sale, even though he hadn't worked much.
- For the good friends life has given him.
- For having family close by.

- For the health of Moroni, Abby, and Mahonri.
- For having a peaceful day at home.
- For my mom, who helped me edit my book.
- For the delicious nopales my mother-in-law made.

- For their pets, Peluche and Maya.
- Because mom listens to her.
- Because she has a bedroom... that's not on fire!
- For making people happy by singing in the school choir.

- For having many talents.
- For her little brother Moroni.
- For going to school.
- For having food, a home, a bedroom, toys, and a swing.

- For mom and dad.
- For milk and quesadillas.

143

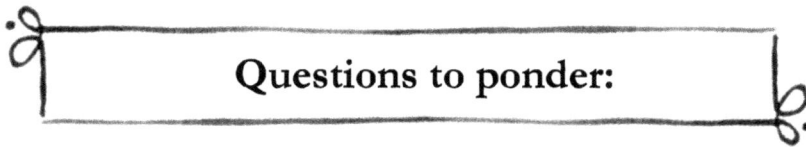

Questions to ponder:

1. Do you regularly give thanks to those around you—and to God?

2. Are you humble enough to recognize that everything you receive and have comes from God?

3. Does your heart fill with joy for the small, everyday blessings?

4. Do you get frustrated easily when you don't have what others have?

5. Do you often compare yourself to others—their resources, families, talents, or skills?

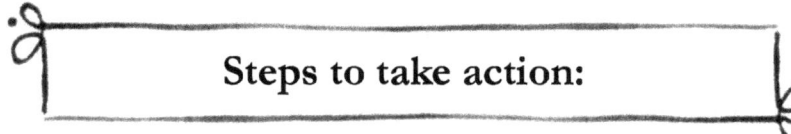

Steps to take action:

1. Write down something you're thankful for every day.
Take a few minutes each day to reflect on the blessings you've received.

2. Say a prayer of pure gratitude.
Pray without asking for anything—just thank God for all that you have.

3. Notice acts of kindness and service from others—and acknowledge them.
Don't miss the opportunity to thank someone for their support.

4. When you're feeling frustrated, take a deep breath and find the good in the situation.
It will help shift your mood and perspective.

5. Do something to express your gratitude.
Write a note, make a phone call, or do something kind to show appreciation to someone in your life.

CHAPTER 9

ESSENTIAL MACRONUTRIENTS FOR THE SOUL

"Beloved, I wish above all things that
thou mayest prosper and be in health,
even as thy soul prospereth."

- 3 John 1:2

Macronutrients are the main components of our diet: proteins, carbohydrates, and fats.

These nutrients provide the energy and elements our bodies need to function properly. Each one plays an important role in our health—repairing tissues, maintaining hormonal balance, and fueling our daily activities.

In the same way, our spirit also requires **"nutrients"**—such as faith, gratitude, hope, and love. Many people have asked me why I'm always smiling, how I manage to find time for so many things, and how I keep up the energy to fulfill my responsibilities.

It's true that I always try to stay joyful—but yes, I've cried, I've yelled, and I've fallen—again and again and again.

What makes me strong and resilient, what fills me with joy, is that after each fall, I've gotten back up. Often with tears in my eyes and a tired heart—but always with the desire to move forward.

In this chapter, I want to share with you the things I do to find happiness and stay positive, even in my lowest moments. I consider these practices the **"essential macronutrients"** for the soul. These habits have helped me physically, emotionally, and spiritually, and I share them with the hope that they'll help you stay strong in your times of trial too.

A Song from the Heart

"Speaking to one another with psalms, hymns and songs from the Spirit. Sing and make music from your heart to the Lord." -Ephesians 5:19

The first essential macronutrient for the soul I want to talk about is music—but I'm referring to uplifting music, such as hymns, worship songs, and praises.

Music has been a refuge in my darkest days. There are songs that inspire, that comfort, that lift the soul. Sometimes a melody brings tears, releasing the emotions that we've been holding in. Music has an incredible power to heal the soul.

I've often found that my spirit connects deeply with music. There's something special about songs that calm the soul, lift the mood, and draw us inward to reflect and connect.

Some songs have resonated with me so deeply that they've become more than melodies—they've become personal hymns, sung prayers that express what words alone cannot. Certain songs have allowed me to communicate with God in a unique way.

While listening or singing them, I often feel my soul open, finding strength and peace. It's as if God uses music to speak directly to me, reminding me I am never alone—that He is always with me.

These songs also become forms of worship, gratitude, and prayer. Some lyrics feel as if they were written just for me—for my situation, my struggles, and my victories.

As I mentioned earlier, I've discovered that music can shift my entire emotional state in an instant. Lately, I've loved going on long runs—sometimes over an hour—and do you know what I do during that time?

I listen to one of my favorite playlists. It helps me disconnect from the world. These songs fill me with joy, peace, and renewed energy, allowing me to face the day with a brighter, more positive mindset.

I'd love to share my playlist with you—just scan the code. It includes Christian songs, hymns, and worship music from various artists and faiths.

scan the QR code
To listen to my favorite playlist!

I am a member of The Church of Jesus Christ of Latter-day Saints, but that doesn't mean I only listen to music from my own religion. I know that other churches and faiths have beautiful music that honors God and Jesus Christ. And I know that just as the hymns of my own faith comfort me, other Christian songs can do the same.

I once shared this playlist with a close friend who was going through a very difficult time. She later told me she listened to those songs all the time, and they became an anchor for her faith and hope.

That made me reflect: we all have different tastes and ways of connecting with our inner selves and with our Heavenly Father. The key is to find the kind of music that fills you, lifts you, and allows you to feel His love.

I encourage you to explore, to search, and to create your own playlist—one filled with songs that renew your strength, bring you light in dark moments, and turn your pain into sung prayers.

Especially during the times when my son Moroni was hospitalized, the drive between our home and the hospital was long—about 45 minutes each way.

Those drives were filled with emotion: sadness at the difficult day ahead, pain because I had to leave my other young children at home. They needed me too, and often didn't want me to leave. My heart felt torn—pulled between my responsibilities as a mother and my desire to be fully present for each of my children.

During those drives, alone in the car, I would play my playlist. The songs did something magical inside me. While driving, I would cry and sing at the same time. Tears would flow as the music filled the car. It was my way of expressing gratitude, pain, and faith to

God. Through those songs, I felt accompanied, strengthened, and renewed. There was one song in particular that, at the time, was the only one that gave me strength. I don't listen to it as much anymore, because I've found others that resonate more with me now.

But back then, that song was the only one that pierced my soul and lifted me up. It's called **"I Will Go and Do,"** written by Nik Day. It's included in the playlist I mentioned, but you can also search for it on any audio or video platform—there are many versions available.

This song shares a powerful message: no matter where we are, the Savior is always by our side. In adversity, we are blessed by Him. And it boldly declares:

"I will go and do. I will stand for truth. Though the world may shut Him out, I will make Him room. I know if I follow Him, follow Him in faith,He will ease my burdens and He'll provide a way. He'll provide a way."

(Song: I Will Go and Do by Nik Day, 2020) © by Intellectual Reserve, Inc.

Singing those words felt like I was telling my Heavenly Father that I was willing to do whatever He asked of me—with faith and determination. The song reminds us that He will give us the strength we need, that He will lift us in our hardest moments, and that in the end, He will provide.

I remember playing that song over and over—singing it loudly as a way to affirm my commitment to God, giving Him my burdens and my life. As I sang, I could feel the love of His Son, Jesus Christ, filling my heart. That song helped me remember that no matter how hard my day would be, I would obey and keep moving forward with faith—knowing I was not alone. Another song I recently discovered is by the artist Lauren Daigle.

She has many songs I love, but one in particular is called **"Thank God I Do"** (Daigle, 2023).

This song is all about gratitude. It says that even though life can be difficult and burdens heavy, with God's help, the load becomes lighter.

The message is powerful: because of God, we find strength, hope, and companionship. What I love most is the chorus. It sinks deep into my heart and soul. I too can say, with absolute certainty: I don't know where I'd be without God by my side.

The singer repeats that she would probably fall apart without Him—and I feel exactly the same way. That chorus has become a prayer of gratitude that I lift up to God. It reminds me how much I rely on Him in every part of my life—and how His love and guidance have shaped every step I've taken.

It's like a motto and a prayer of gratitude that I lift up to God, recognizing that thanks to Him, I am still standing and moving forward. This reflection makes me realize how much I depend on Him in every aspect of my life, and how His love and guidance have shaped every step I take.

I had the opportunity to hear a speaker who shared his experience of living in China many years ago. He explained that during the Christmas season, you could hear familiar Christmas music in the malls, but also melodies of popular religious hymns—though only the melody, without the lyrics. He invited us to reflect: why would they remove the lyrics? Do you have any idea why? In that country, Christianity is a minority. And religious hymns carry special power. The words they contain testify of the mission of the Savior Jesus Christ: His birth, His life, and His resurrection. These words are a source of light and hope. They are a living testimony that God lives, that He loves us, and that He hears us. The vast majority of religious hymns affirm the joy we feel when we keep the commandments and remind us that even when we make mistakes, we can be forgiven and find peace through His grace.

The lyrics of music can deeply influence our decisions. When I was very young, I did my best to remain faithful to God's commandments. I must have been about 15 years old, and I remember being in a situation where I had to decide whether to stay true to my promises to Him or break them. That decision was so important that it could have completely changed the course of my life.

Do you know what helped me decide? The lyrics of a hymn.

That hymn spoke about being faithful to God and fulfilling the sacred duties He has given us. The song is called **"I Love to See the Temple."** It reminded me of my goal and strengthened my convictions. Just like Joseph, who was sold into Egypt and chose to flee from sin, I also ran from that situation and never found myself in anything like it again. It was an experience that taught me that God is more important than any carnal desire I might have.

The course of my life changed because of a hymn. Thanks to that personal testimony, now in my home we play uplifting music every day so that my children can memorize those words and remember them in moments when they need courage and strength.

If you don't have this habit yet and feel the need to nourish your spirit, I invite you to search for, listen to, and sing hymns and spiritual songs. It doesn't matter if you don't have a beautiful voice; what matters is allowing the music to strengthen your soul.

"Music is a beautiful and glorious gift
from God, and nothing can equal it.
Music drives away the devil and makes
people joyful; it is a spiritual comfort and
a bond between God and man."

- Martin Luther

Questions to ponder:

1. What songs touch my soul deeply, and why?

2. What feelings do I experience when I sing hymns and worship songs?

3. When was the last time I sang with a heart full of gratitude or emotion?

4. How has uplifting music impacted my relationship with God and my personal well-being?

5. Can I identify a song or hymn that helped me during a difficult time?

Steps to take action:

1. Choose a hymn or song that inspires you and reflect on its lyrics—what it makes you feel and how you can apply its message in your life.

2. Create a playlist with hymns, worship songs, or uplifting music, and listen to it regularly to strengthen your spirit.

3. Use free moments—like when you're running, driving, cooking, or cleaning—to listen to melodies that lift your mood and deepen your faith.

4. Memorize the lyrics of your favorite hymns or songs and sing them when you need strength or peace.

5. Set aside time to learn new hymns or songs that will expand your spiritual playlist and enrich your connection with God.

Service

"Whoever is kind to the poor lends to the Lord, and he will reward them for what they have done." -Proverbs 19:17

Another essential macronutrient to nourish our soul is service. This topic can be challenging for many, as we often find ourselves in situations where we feel like we are the ones in need of help. However, God, in His infinite wisdom, teaches us through His word that when we focus on helping others, we also find solutions and relief for our own difficulties.

In **Matthew 25:40,** Jesus tells us: **"Truly I tell you, whatever you did for one of the least of these brothers and sisters of mine, you did for me."** This scripture reminds us that every act of kindness and service toward others is, in reality, an act of love toward God Himself.

However, I've noticed a remarkable difference when I choose to look beyond myself. When I decide to think about others and give of my time, something magical happens. It's as if a deep power fills me, helping me forget my problems and offering me new hope. The act of serving others brings me clarity, peace, and unexpected blessings. I feel happier, more useful—like an instrument in God's hands. And that connection, that certainty that He is using me to bless others, fills me with incomparable joy. Because when we serve, God multiplies our strength.

Service lifts us spiritually and helps us see life from a wider perspective. Through service, we learn empathy, gratitude, and humility, and we strengthen our relationship with God. He blesses us abundantly when we stop focusing only on our own burdens and choose to reach out to someone else.

I want to invite you to include service in your daily life, no matter how small. It might be a kind gesture, a word of encouragement, or simply being present for someone in need. Every act of service matters, and as the Lord promised, when we give, we also receive.

I have been deeply blessed by the service I've received during times of discouragement. Wonderful people have become earthly angels—offering me support, comfort, and strength when I needed it most. That selfless service didn't just help me overcome trials—it planted in me a genuine desire to give that same love and support to others facing their own struggles.

Moreover, the trials I've lived through have helped me develop attributes and qualities I didn't have before. I've learned to be more empathetic, understanding, and patient. Now, when I see someone going through challenges, I feel I can offer more than just words—I can share my experience, my compassion, and most of all, my willingness to help.

I firmly believe that our trials not only shape us, but they also prepare us to be an outstretched hand to others. I consider it a privilege to help others because in doing so, I feel I'm fulfilling the purpose God has for me.

Recently, I was deeply worried about some health problems my children were facing. I was overwhelmed, my mind filled with uncertainty about what could happen and how I could fix it. But I felt a strong impression—I needed to visit some elderly women from my church. Even though I didn't have much time, I set aside a moment in my schedule and, along with my children, we baked homemade bread. It was a small gesture, but we did it with love.

We brought the bread to them, and the experience turned out to be more strengthening than I could have imagined. I was so focused on my own struggles, on my world full of worries, that I couldn't see beyond my own bubble. But when I arrived at the first woman's home, everything changed. I realized her situation was far more complicated than mine—she lived alone, without her children, struggled to walk for fear of falling, and had very little support. Hearing about her hardships made me realize how blessed my life truly is.

Then we visited another woman, and to my surprise, she too was facing major challenges. She told us about her health issues and how hard it was for her to eat properly. It was eye-opening to realize her pain and limitations.

When we left both homes, my husband and I looked at each other and felt the same thing: our life is perfect. We have so much to be thankful for. There are so many people in the world facing greater challenges than we are, and service not only helps them—it also heals and strengthens our own hearts.

Since childhood, I had great examples of service thanks to my mother and grandmother. For as long as I can remember, they were always helping others—children, youth, and adults. They gave not only financially, but also their time and skills. I grew up surrounded by those examples of love and generosity, and that taught me the value of giving without expecting anything in return.

I also learned to love service during my mission. As I mentioned at the beginning of this book, I served as a missionary for The

Church of Jesus Christ of Latter-day Saints, and that experience was truly invaluable. I realized that when I helped others—without seeking anything in return—I received genuine happiness, love from strangers, and deep satisfaction.

One of the most tangible blessings I've experienced is how God multiplies my time. I know exactly what I can typically accomplish in 24 hours—but each day is filled with important tasks: helping my kids with therapy and homework, cooking, supporting them in developing their talents, exercising with them, plus fulfilling household responsibilities.

However, I've witnessed the miracles that happen when we choose to serve. I feel like my time stretches—tasks become more manageable, I'm able to finish them more quickly, or sometimes God brings the right people into my life to help me.

That's why I encourage you not to fall into the trap of thinking that dedicating time to serve God's children will slow you down or keep you from your own goals or responsibilities. The opposite is true. It's as if God transforms our efforts and multiplies our capacity, allowing us to move forward far more than we could have on our own.

There's a story in **1 Kings 17:8–16** that tells of the prophet Elijah and a widow in Zarephath during a time of great famine.

God told Elijah to go to Zarephath, where He had commanded a widow to feed him. When Elijah arrived at the town's entrance, he found a woman gathering sticks. He asked her for a little water, and as she went to get it, he also asked for a piece of bread.

The widow replied:

"As surely as the Lord your God lives," she replied, "I don't have any bread—only a handful of flour in a jar and a little olive oil in a jug. I am gathering a few sticks to take home and make a meal for myself and my son, that we may eat it—and die." (1 Kings 17:12)

Elijah told her not to be afraid and to do as she said—but to first make him a small loaf of bread, then prepare something for herself and her son. Then he gave her this promise:

"For this is what the Lord, the God of Israel, says: 'The jar of flour will not be used up and the jug of oil will not run dry until the day the Lord sends rain on the land.'"(1 Kings 17:14)

The woman obeyed, and just as Elijah had said, the flour and oil did not run out during the entire famine. She, her family, and Elijah had enough to eat every day—thanks to God's miraculous provision.

This story shows us that God's calculations go beyond our human logic and limitations. Even though the widow only had enough for one more day, when she acted in faith and generosity, she experienced a miracle that sustained her and her son.

When we give of the little we have—time, resources, love, or skills—God takes our offering, multiplies it, and blesses us in miraculous ways. Just as the flour and oil never ran out, our lives can be filled and sustained when we trust in God's divine promise.

Serve one another humbly in **Love**

Galatians 5:13

"May we show our love and appreciation for the Savior's atoning sacrifice through our simple, compassionate acts of service."

- M. Russell Ballard

Questions to ponder:

1. When was the last time you performed an act of service, and how did it make you feel?

2. Recall a time in your life when someone did something meaningful for you. How did it impact your life and emotions?

3. Is there someone close to you who could benefit from your help—whether emotionally, physically, or spiritually?

4. How can you incorporate service into your daily life to strengthen your relationships and your community?

Steps to take action:

1. Start with small acts of service, such as calling a loved one, sending a message of encouragement, or taking time to listen to someone in need.

2. Offer practical help in your home or community—prepare a meal for someone, or watch a friend's children for a few hours.

3. Take time to understand the needs of those around you and find specific ways you can help.

4. Commit to performing at least one meaningful act of service each week, and keep a record to reflect on how it makes you feel.

5. Pray for guidance and inspiration to know who you can serve and how to do it with a heart full of love and charity.

Studying the Word of God Daily

"Keep this Book of the Law always on your lips; meditate on it day and night, so that you may be careful to do everything written in it. Then you will be prosperous and successful." - **Josué 1:8**

On my phone, I have access to an app called Gospel Library. I imagine there are many other free apps you can download as well. Since Moroni came into our lives, I've discovered I have certain keywords that keep coming up for me—my own spiritual search terms.

Do you want to know what my keywords have been over the years? Affliction, trials, challenges, faith, hope, miracles, strength, patience, perseverance, trust, and gratitude.

What I do is type these words into the search bar, and the app shows me scriptures and inspiring messages related to those topics. Doing this has helped me clear up doubts, gain understanding, and fill myself with the faith and hope I've needed most.

These sacred writings were recorded by prophets inspired by God. As it says in **2 Peter 1:21:**

"For prophecy never had its origin in the human will, but prophets, though human, spoke from God as they were carried along by the Holy Spirit."

Even though the scriptures were written hundreds of years ago and some of the stories may seem far removed from us, they are still relevant today. Back then, followers of Christ faced physical wars, but today we face spiritual ones. The lessons found in scripture can be a powerful guide in our everyday battles.

As **Ephesians 6:12** reminds us:

"For we wrestle not against flesh and blood, but against principalities, against powers, against the rulers of the darkness of this world, against spiritual wickedness in high places."

Scriptures are a source of strength, direction, and hope as we face the visible and invisible battles of life.

Personally, one of the reasons I love studying the scriptures daily is because they help me remember what I already know. These are truths I've heard since I was a little girl. Though the gospel doesn't change, as humans, we tend to forget quickly. That's why we learn through repetition. In any area of life, if we want to master something, we need to practice and review it constantly until it really sinks into our minds and hearts.

Now that I'm an adult and life is so busy, I often forget to do the things I know I should do. But daily scripture study helps me remember those important truths, relive the feelings they bring me, and reflect on the experiences I've had. Through the scriptures, I recognize areas where I need to grow and the Christlike attributes I must develop to follow Jesus Christ and one day return to my Heavenly Father.

Something I've learned over time is that we shouldn't wait until we're in the middle of a trial to seek God and His word. Preparation for life's challenges begins much earlier—with small, daily acts: prayer, scripture study, quiet reflection, and constant seeking of His guidance. Over time, this consistency builds a solid foundation that will sustain us when life's storms come.

This reminds me of the story of the wise and foolish builders in **Matthew 7:24–27:**

"Therefore everyone who hears these words of mine and puts them into practice is like a wise man who built his house on the rock. The rain came down, the streams rose, and the winds blew and beat against that house; yet it did not fall, because it had its foundation on the rock. But everyone who hears these words of mine and does not put them into practice is like a foolish man who built his house on sand. The rain came down, the streams rose, and the winds blew and beat against that house, and it fell with a great crash."

The foolish man built his house on sand because it was quicker and easier. Maybe he was too busy with worldly things to take time to strengthen his spiritual foundation. But when the storms came, his house fell because it lacked a solid base.

In contrast, the wise man built his house on the rock. Before anything else, he prioritized the essential things—his family, quality time, scripture study, prayer, service, church attendance, and strengthening his faith. When the storms came, his house stood firm because it was supported by a solid foundation.

I encourage you to create a daily habit of seeking God. Start with small steps: a short prayer, reading one verse, and meditating on its meaning. Gradually, increase the time and depth of your study. That time with God is invaluable—it strengthens our connection with Him and prepares us to face challenges with greater strength.

This also ties in with the parable of the ten virgins in **Matthew 25:1–13**. Jesus tells how ten young women waited for the bridegroom with their lamps, which needed enough oil to stay lit. Five of them were wise and brought extra oil, while the other five were foolish and did not. When the call came to meet the bridegroom, the foolish ones realized they didn't have enough oil and asked the wise ones to share. But the wise virgins replied: **"No, they replied, 'there may not be enough for both us and you. Instead, go to those who sell oil and buy some for yourselves." (Matthew 25:9).**

At first, this might seem selfish or unkind. But while the foolish ones went to buy oil, the bridegroom arrived, and the wise ones entered with him to the wedding banquet—and the door was shut. When the others returned, they cried out to enter, but he answered: **"But he replied, 'Truly I tell you, I don't know you." (Matthew 25:12).**

This parable teaches us that the wise virgins weren't being selfish—they were showing us that there are things we simply can't give to others: spiritual strength, faith, and our personal relationship with God. As much as we'd love to give our faith to someone else, it's something they must develop themselves.

The wise virgins' response is, to me, a message of concern, encouragement, and an invitation to act—just like we do when we share our testimony with others.

God has called us to serve, to lift the hands that hang down, to pray for others, to inspire, and to share our light. But each person has the responsibility to prepare their own lamp and fill their own reservoir of faith and spiritual strength.

Build your life on the rock of Jesus Christ and keep your lamps filled with oil. These daily actions will make all the difference—in both peaceful days and stormy ones.

Just like a map leads us to our destination, the scriptures guide us safely into the arms of our Heavenly Father.

Search the scriptures: for in them ye think ye have ETERNAL LIFE: and they are they which testify of ME

John 5:39

Questions to ponder:

1. How often do you read the scriptures? Do you feel it's enough to build a solid faith and stay spiritually strong?

2. What are some of your favorite scriptures, and what inspires or motivates you most about them?

3. Can you recall a time in your life when you felt touched by the Spirit while reading the scriptures? How did that experience impact your life?

4. What obstacles have prevented you from reading the scriptures daily, and how could you overcome them to make study a consistent habit?

5. How can you share what you're learning from the scriptures with others?

Steps to take action:

1. Set a specific time: Choose a time of day—morning or bedtime—to read the scriptures, even if it's just for 5–10 minutes.

2. Pick a passage or theme: Focus on a specific book or topic in the scriptures and read with intent. Write down your thoughts or impressions in a journal.

3. Study with purpose: Read with a question or situation in mind and seek answers or guidance through the scriptures.

4. Memorize a verse: Choose one verse each week that inspires you and commit it to memory. Reflect on how to apply it to your daily life.

5. Listen to the scriptures: On busy days, use audio tools to listen to scripture passages while driving, cooking, or doing chores.

6. Share what you've learned: Take time to share with your family, friends, or community what you've learned from your scripture study and how it has blessed your life.

7. Pray before and after reading: Ask for guidance before you begin reading and give thanks afterward for the impressions and teachings you received.

Exercise

"But those who hope in the Lord will renew their strength. They will soar on wings like eagles; they will run and not grow weary, they will walk and not be faint." - Isaías 40:31

God created our bodies and declared in the Bible that our bodies are temples where His Spirit dwells. In 1 Corinthians 3:16–17, we are solemnly reminded:

"Don't you know that you yourselves are God's temple and that God's Spirit dwells in your midst? If anyone destroys God's temple, God will destroy that person; for God's temple is sacred, and you together are that temple."

This passage shows that our body is not just a physical structure, but a sacred creation—a perfect temple designed by the hands of God.

For this reason, I believe healing the soul and spirit is deeply connected to caring for our bodies. The body is the vessel that holds our spirit—the dwelling place of God's Spirit. It's a responsibility He has given us, and caring for it doesn't only mean feeding it well, but also strengthening it through exercise.

When we exercise and care for our bodies, we're strengthening not just our muscles, but also every organ and even our brain. A balanced body helps us stay in communion with our spirit and have a deeper connection with God.

If we want to be in harmony with the Spirit, we must treat our body with the same reverence we would treat a sacred temple. By doing so, we honor our Creator and His perfect work.

Four years ago, I started an intense training program that combines functional movements like weightlifting and cardiovascular activity. At the time, Moroni was just a 6-month-old baby whose health demanded my full attention. I wasn't ready to start a new workout program, and the timing wasn't ideal, but I chose to trust myself and my ability to persevere.

I committed to not skipping a single class. Over time, I discovered that exercise helped me on a much deeper level: it allowed me to overcome negative emotions and release the emotional weight I was carrying. Exercise became an outlet for all the sadness, anxiety, and frustration I had built up—transforming them into strength and resilience.

Many times, when I've felt discouraged or unmotivated, when I've had no desire to exercise, the only reason I've shown up is because it had already become a habit. My morning gym routine has helped me stay focused and better manage emotional burdens.

Once, I was holding in so many emotions because Moroni wasn't progressing, and it must have shown on my face. When I arrived at class, my trainer asked if I was okay, and I couldn't hold it in—I broke down in tears. She hugged me and encouraged me to do the workout. By the time I finished, everything felt different. A heavy emotional burden had lifted, and I felt a deep sense of relief and freedom.

What happened in that one hour that made me feel so different? That gym time was a gift to myself. I disconnected from my responsibilities as a mom, stepped away from daily worries, and gave myself permission to focus entirely on me.

There's even a scientific explanation for this: when we exercise, our brain produces more dopamine, serotonin, and endorphins—neurotransmitters that help reduce stress, anxiety, and symptoms of depression, allowing us to experience a greater sense of happiness.

Moving our bodies not only strengthens our muscles and improves physical health, but also acts as a powerful tool for emotional regulation. It helps us release tension, boosts our self-esteem, and increases our overall sense of well-being.

Each workout is a reminder that we are strong and capable, enabling us to face daily challenges with a more positive and resilient mindset.

I encourage you to try incorporating exercise into your daily routine—even if it's hard at first. You'll soon find it's a powerful way to release stress, refocus your energy, and find balance in the midst of life's challenges.

I've realized how much exercise has helped me feel stronger and more capable. I've accomplished things I once thought impossible—like lifting weights with a barbell, doing pull-ups, and even climbing a rope to the top. It's made me feel powerful, energized, and full of confidence.

These small victories have transformed how I see myself and taught me to recognize the strength I have as a daughter of God. Now, I feel like a better version of the person I've always wanted to become.

Recently, I've also ventured into the world of running. I recently completed a 10K run—something I once saw as a distant dream. Every kilometer, every small accomplishment, has become a stepping stone that has strengthened my self-esteem and confidence, both as a mother and as a woman.

So nowadays, whenever I feel sad or discouraged, my remedy—or better said, my medicine—is to go for a run. During those runs, I release all the negative emotions and emotional weight I carry. It's a physical and mental release that brings clarity and leaves me feeling renewed.

As I mentioned earlier, I listen to uplifting songs while I run. And in those moments, I genuinely feel that God is running alongside me, cheering me on, saying, **"You can do this."** By the end of the run, those words echo so strongly in my mind that I believe them—I tell myself, **"I can overcome this."**

Do not be wise
in your own eyes;
fear the Lord,
and shun evil.
This will bring
health to
your body
and nourishment
to your bones.

PROVERBS 3:7-8

That's what I want to invite you to do: if you don't yet have this habit in your life, don't worry—it's never too late to start. There's no age limit or perfect time. I invite you to start today by taking small steps. I've learned that to build and maintain a habit, we shouldn't begin with goals that are too big or overwhelming, as that can discourage us. Instead, start with what's within your reach—small, manageable changes.

Remember that we're all in different stages of life with unique circumstances. For some, walking 30 minutes might be a major challenge, while for others it's easy. What matters is not comparing yourself to others, because each of us lives with unique emotional, physical, or financial realities.

Do the best you can within your own circumstances. Find even a little bit of time to move and take care of yourself. Whether it's walking, running, biking, or following dance videos on YouTube, there are many tools available. What's important is simply to start. Every small step counts, and over time, those small efforts lead to big changes.

I remember a conversation I once had with a sister from church when I only had Abby and Mahonri as little ones. She talked about how important it is for mothers to take time for themselves—even something as simple as relaxing in a warm bath. At the time, her advice seemed completely unrealistic. I told her it was impossible—that I didn't have time for myself because I had to care for my children. I truly believed that being a good mother meant sacrificing everything for them. But with time and experience, I realized how mistaken I was.

Over time, I learned that in order to be the best mother I could be, I first had to care for myself. I discovered that when I prioritize my physical, emotional, and mental health—when I exercise and find ways to process negative emotions—I become a better version of myself for my children. This shift in mindset helped me understand that loving and caring for myself is not selfish, but rather a way to strengthen my ability to be a present, loving, and patient mother. It has also increased my capacity to meet my responsibilities and to be more generous and compassionate with others.

Thanks to exercise, my kids have enjoyed having an active, playful mom—because I have the energy and stamina to run, jump, chase them, and carry them. It's created unforgettable memories for all of us. I can join them in activities like riding bikes, playing **"monster"** around the house, or crawling through narrow tunnels at amusement parks. I feel so grateful to be able to do this because I've worked hard on my health and physical strength. I've noticed I'm one of the few moms who jumps in to play with her kids, climbs, slides, crouches, and keeps up with their pace. That wouldn't be possible without consistent exercise.

My husband is also a great example—we work out together. For us, it's a special time we enjoy as a couple. I've seen how strong he is. Last year, for example, we took a road trip through several states. Along the way, we visited three national parks that required long and challenging hikes. I was amazed to see my husband carrying Moroni on his back in a child carrier for hours. On those hikes—steep, rocky paths—he carried Moroni the whole way, allowing him to enjoy our family adventure.

It's essential for my husband to have the physical strength to help Moroni enjoy our family outings and to spend quality time with our kids. He has just as much energy as I do to keep moving, stay active, and continue playing with them.

Having physical strength has also helped me carry Moroni without injuring myself, hold him during a crisis without losing control, and assist him during therapy. It's helped me rock him, dress him, and keep up with his energy—because he doesn't recognize boundaries. It helps me lift him when he falls, help him up the stairs, or get him in the car. I often have to carry him for long periods when he feels anxious or unsafe, and if my body weren't strong, it would be even more exhausting.

Moroni is now four years old, but developmentally, he's like a much younger child. His body is big and heavy. I can't imagine how much he'll weigh in a few years, but I know I need to be ready. That's why I push myself to stay active and build physical strength—because my endurance isn't just for me, it's for Moroni and the support he'll need in the future.

So I encourage you to make that extra effort. Do it for yourself, for your well-being, and for your family. It's a habit that takes commitment and planning, but I know that when you look back, you'll realize it was one of the best decisions you could've made. You'll feel more joy, positivity, and energy to face life—and you'll be amazed at all you can achieve as a mother or father, grandparent, homemaker, student, entrepreneur, professional, caregiver, or whatever role you fill.

Your well-being is a priceless investment. Start today!

Questions to ponder:

1.   How often do you engage in physical activity, and how do you feel it impacts your daily well-being?

2.   What types of exercise make you feel the most energized and happy, and why do you think that is?

3.   Can you recall a time when exercise helped you manage stress or overcome negative emotions?

4.   What obstacles do you face in maintaining a consistent exercise routine, and how could you overcome them?

5.   How do you think regular exercise could improve other areas of your life, such as concentration, creativity, or personal relationships?

Steps to take action:

1. Set a daily schedule—even just 10–15 minutes—for physical activity.

2. Choose an activity you enjoy (like walking, running, dancing, or yoga) and make it a habit.

3. Track your progress in a journal or app to stay motivated and see your improvement.

4. Find a workout partner or join a group to share the experience and support one another.

5. Set small, achievable goals, and celebrate each milestone, no matter how minor, to reinforce your commitment.

CHAPTER 10

SHARE WHAT YOU HOLD IN YOUR HEART

"A good man brings good things out of
the good stored up in his heart, and an
evil man brings evil things out of the evil
stored up in his heart. For the mouth
speaks what the heart is full of."

- Luke 6:45

Each of us is unique. Have you ever stopped to think that our fingerprints are perfectly designed and no two are alike? In the same way, our virtues, gifts, and personalities are also unique. Just as our experiences on earth are different, each of us faces different challenges, learns unique lessons, and has a special voice. These differences are what make life meaningful. That's why each of us has a unique identity and mission, and our experiences and knowledge are of great value to others. Everything you've lived and learned is important to share. It's no coincidence that God sent you to earth and placed certain people in your life. God asks us to open our mouths, to share, and to help others.

"Our spiritual experiences are like beacons that light our path, guiding us toward sure and steady steps."

We can all help others. We can all lift up the hands that hang down. We can all testify of God's goodness. It's sad to think that our flaws and mistakes make us unworthy of sharing anything—especially about God. But if you ever feel that way, remember it is a lie from Satan. He deceives us into believing we're not enough or that our voice has nothing meaningful to offer.

Maybe others will think our efforts or words aren't good enough, but as long as we do our best, that will be enough. I've felt that insecurity many times myself, but I've learned to accept that it's okay to make mistakes. What matters is trying with a sincere heart and trusting that God can use our imperfections to accomplish His work.

I invite you to share what's in your heart. For many years, I kept all the experiences I've shared here tucked away in my heart. But the time came when God told me it was time to share, and I did. I'm so grateful I did, because as I wrote and re-read my words, my own testimony of God grew stronger. Remembering the experiences I've lived with my family helps me see that God has always been there—along with His Son, Jesus Christ.

He said to them,
Go into all the world and

preach the
gospel.

Mark 16:15

Write down what you feel. And if you're not ready to share it yet, keep writing. The day will come when those words will strengthen you in the future—or bless your children, your grandchildren, or a friend.

Deuteronomy 8:2–3

"Remember how the Lord your God led you all the way in the wilderness these forty years, to humble and test you in order to know what was in your heart, whether or not you would keep his commands. He humbled you, causing you to hunger and then feeding you with manna, which neither you nor your ancestors had known, to teach you that man does not live on bread alone but on every word that comes from the mouth of the Lord."

When I read this verse, it deeply moved me because it refers to an incredibly difficult time in the life of the Israelites. In short, God had freed them from slavery in Egypt, but they spent 40 years in the wilderness facing trials and challenges. During that time, many of them complained about their afflictions.

I want to invite you to reflect on these words and read them slowly—applying them to yourself.

"Remember how the Lord your God led you all the way in the wilderness these forty years..." It's as if these words were directed to me:

"Remember, Gabby, how the Lord your God led you these four years since Moroni arrived."

The verse continues:**"...to humble and test you in order to know what was in your heart, whether or not you would keep his commands."** And yes, He did. God allowed me to face afflictions so I could learn humility. He tested me so that, through the refining fire, I would become a stronger woman—with greater faith and more love in my heart. He wanted to see what was within me, if I would obey and remain faithful even in the hardest times. Then it says:

"He humbled you, causing you to hunger and then feeding you with manna, which neither you nor your ancestors had known..."

In my case, I hungered for comfort. I felt darkness, pain, loneliness, and a lack of strength. Many times, I became desperate. I fell again and again. But even so, God sustained me in ways I had never known. That manna, that heavenly nourishment, came in the form of moments of light, personal revelation, divine comfort, and His constant presence. That manna, that spiritual food, gave me life—again and again.

A life that, despite the trials, we have lived fully. Because now my faith has become certainty—absolute knowledge. Today I know, without any doubt, that God is real. I know He has sustained me, taken me by the hand, and will lead me back to His presence in His heavenly mansion.

That's why I felt in my heart the need to share my story— perhaps just to help you remember what you already know and remind you that God loves you. You, too, can be touched by heaven, embraced by divine arms, and filled with the power needed to overcome any obstacle.

Use your voice to inspire, your hands to embrace, your heart to love, and your strength to lift someone else.

Questions to ponder:

1. Do you feel like you share your experiences and testimony with others as often as you'd like?

2. What holds you back from opening your mouth and sharing what you know about God? Is it fear, insecurity, or lack of opportunity?

3. How do you feel when you share God's word with someone?

4. What kind of impact do you believe your words and actions can have on those around you?

5. Do you have examples in your life of people who have been blessed because you shared your testimony or your faith?

6. What personal experiences or lessons do you think could inspire or help others?

Steps to take action:

1. If you find it hard to speak, start by sharing short faith messages on social media—such as reflections, scriptures, or testimonies about how God has helped you.

2. Memorize scriptures that could be helpful to others and share them naturally when the opportunity arises.

3. Join community or church groups where you can openly share your testimony.

4. Pray for inspiration about who might benefit from hearing your experience or receiving a message of faith.

5. Write down your spiritual experiences in a journal or blog, and consider sharing parts of them with others. Often, our stories resonate with someone going through something similar.

5. Invite someone to attend church or a spiritual event with you.

6. Gift a Bible, an inspiring book, or a hymn to someone who may be seeking hope or spiritual guidance.

FINAL WORDS

This rollercoaster that God allowed me to ride has been incredibly challenging; it has pushed me to my limits, and I've felt deep fear. We've gone through dark tunnels where I could barely see clearly, and I wondered when the tunnel would finally end. But without much warning, and at the most unexpected moment, a small ray of light would appear at the end, and little by little, that light began to illuminate everything in its path. We entered and exited tunnels again and again, and each experience was different—because with each one, we gained experience and wisdom. Little by little, this **"journey-adventure"** became easier to endure, despite the sharp turns that caused us pain. It has been rewarding to see my children and husband united as a family, overcoming these challenges together. Today, we are at the top; we can see the beautiful landscape, all the colors, feel the wind, breathe in the sweet aromas, soak in the rays of the sun, and look back at the path we've traveled—shouting with joy and happiness that we've truly enjoyed the ride. It has all been worth it. Truly, it has been perfect.

I wish I could shout so loudly that my voice would reach every corner of the Earth and say: **God lives!** He is a God of love and perfection. He created us to experience joy, and opposition is a vital part of that joy—bringing it to life in a powerful, real way.

Moroni recently had an appointment with his cardiologist, whom we hadn't seen in a year. Every time we go, I feel nervous—but this time, I went with confidence and faith.

After the electrocardiogram and ultrasound, the cardiologist, Dr. Sureka, came out and told me that Moroni was doing very well. He showed me the same diagram he always does, illustrating the arteries that were repaired, and he said the surgeons had done an excellent job with him.

I should mention that, since he was a baby, every time we visited the cardiologist, he told me that Moroni would need multiple open-heart surgeries because of his lack of elastin. Moroni is now 4 years old and has not needed any further interventions.

I asked the cardiologist, **"Moroni is missing elastin, right?"**

He replied, **"Yes, Moroni doesn't have elastin in his body."**

So I asked again, **"Then how is it possible that his arteries are still okay now that he's growing? How have they stretched if he doesn't have elastin?"**

The cardiologist repeated that the surgeons had done a great job and that Moroni was fine.

And so I ask myself: **How has Moroni been able to keep living without needing another open-heart surgery all these years?**

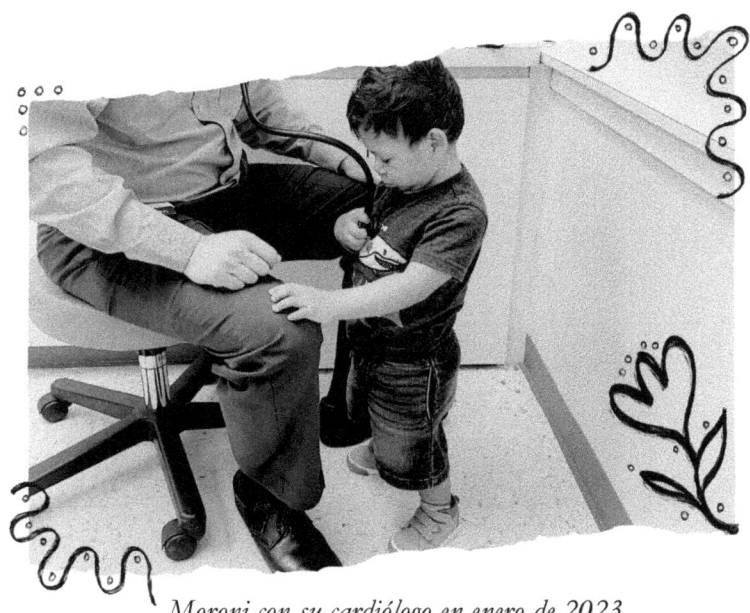

Moroni con su cardiólogo en enero de 2023.

Elastin is crucial for the elasticity of body tissues, such as the arteries, which must expand as a person grows. When Moroni was a baby, his arteries were tiny, and as a result, his blood flow was nearly nonexistent. He was dying. That's why he had open-heart surgery at just 4 months old—to give him a chance to live. During the surgery, they left him with arteries the size of a baby's, and now, at age four, he's still living with those same arteries.

But I know the reason: they are God's miracles in my son's life. Moroni is still alive because he is a miracle; his heart is a miracle.

As a baby, he was also diagnosed with long QT syndrome, a condition that causes irregular heart rhythms and affects the electrical signals that travel through the heart.

This could have led to seizures and, at any moment, death.

However, he was healed—something that medically has no cure. My son's heart is living proof that God still performs miracles. What is most defective in his body is his heart, and yet, ironically, what is most beautiful in him is also his heart.

Last year, I wrote a children's book based on Moroni and Mahonri's life, titled **"My Brother Doesn't Speak, But His Heart Does."** I donated the book to Moroni's school, and the principal approved it.

I had the opportunity to speak with her, and she asked me: **"Do you know what Moroni's name sign is in sign language? It's the same as your book title."**

It's important to note that in Deaf culture, people choose a name sign that identifies you. Then she added, **"I thought you already knew and that's why you chose that title for your book."**

But I didn't know. So she said, **"I'll show you the sign. I'll draw it so you can see."**

The name sign is made by forming the letter M (for Moroni) with the right hand, placing it over the heart, and then opening the hand outward—symbolizing that his heart is full of love and he shares it freely with everyone.

The school principal confirmed to me that I'm not the only one who can testify that Moroni's heart speaks—even if his mouth doesn't say many words.

Moroni's heart was created uniquely—physically affected by congenital heart disease, but spiritually gifted with a divine purpose: to bring joy and love to everyone around him.

1. Form the letter "M" in American Sign Language (ASL).

2. Bring your hand to your heart.

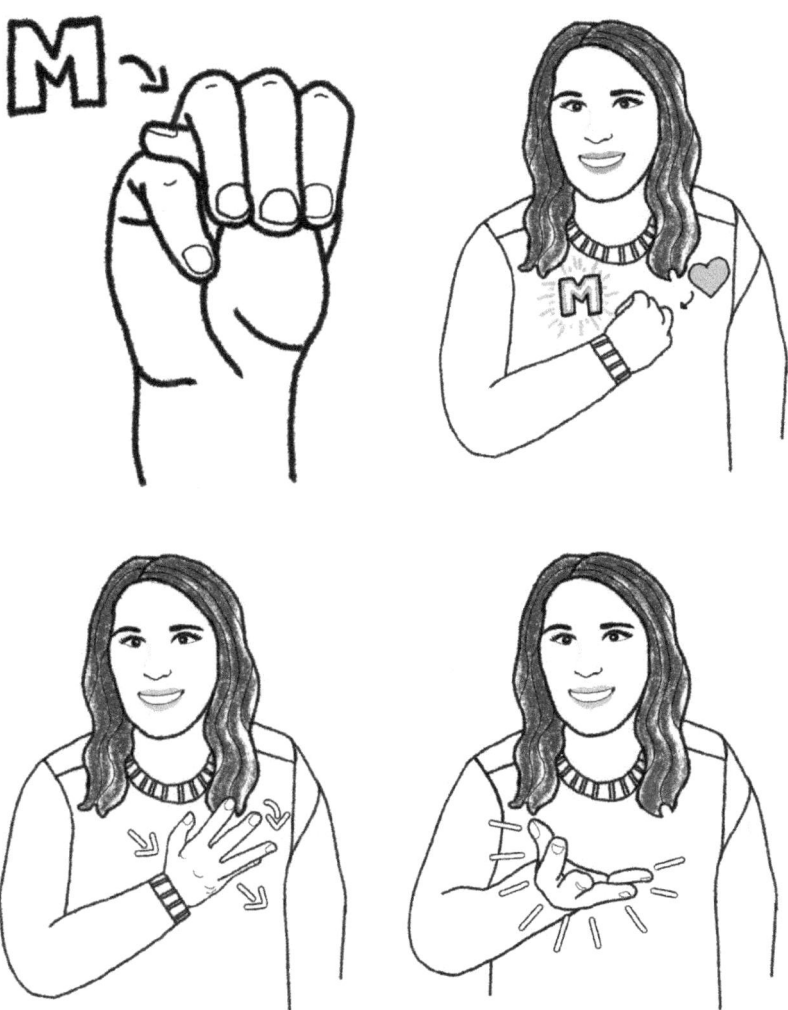

3. Slowly move your hand away from your heart.

4. Open your hand outward.

Did you know that Williams syndrome is also known as the **"happy syndrome"**? Moroni was perfectly created, and that happiness is something many of us need. That's why he was sent just as he is—his smile carries a purity and innocence unlike any other.

I want to thank you for reading this book and for learning about my story. To me, it is something deeply sacred and personal. I hope that through my experiences, you've been able to recognize how God's hand has also been present in your own life.

God loves you and knows you better than you know yourself. He knows everything you are capable of achieving, and for that reason, He gives us experiences that are necessary for our growth. Many of those experiences can be painful, but when faced with faith and trust, they become some of life's greatest treasures.

Remember that we have access to a special guide—a gentle voice: the Holy Spirit. He speaks to us, teaches us, and even warns us. Although everyone has access to Him freely, not everyone benefits from His influence. It requires creating the right environment for Him to dwell with us. Avoid distractions—it is worth it to have His guidance in your life. Let's be more humble to recognize when He is speaking to us, and brave enough to obey His direction.

When we listen with both our heart and mind—and when we obey—we are promised that we will be able to climb the highest mountains and cross the deepest valleys. Your own roller coaster will become a fascinating journey—if you let God ride it with you.

God's plan is for all of us to finish this journey with the final stop at His heavenly home, where we will partake of His endless glory and joy—a place where there will be no afflictions, no illness, and no pain.

Don't give up. Keep trusting, keep asking the Father for help. Continue fighting like a warrior against the enemy, and you will come out victorious in every battle—because angels will be fighting by your side.

Happiness is possible, even in the middle of life's hardest circumstances. Remember, God gave us the greatest gift: His Son, Jesus Christ. He came to give His life for us, to pay for our sins. Because of that sacrifice, we have the chance to try again and again—to get up every time we fall. His light shines upon us and shows us the path we should follow.

Jesus Christ strengthens us. His life was the perfect example we should all follow. I know that if we walk in His footsteps, we will have the spiritual power to overcome any challenge. He taught us a better way to live—a life full of service, love, charity, and humility. He is the way back to the Father, and He has called us to follow Him. Let us renew our commitment to walk in His steps every day of our lives.

Matthew 6:33

"But seek first his kingdom and his righteousness, and all these things will be given to you as well."

Draw closer to God each day through prayer, studying His word, and reading inspired books. Find music that fills your heart, share your gifts, be more grateful, care for your sacred body, and serve others—these things can help you come to know God and Jesus Christ more deeply. They can help you build a foundation as solid and unshakable as a rock.

Sometimes, the miracles God performs depend greatly on what we are willing to do for ourselves and for the things we desire. If we put in the effort and continue seeking, we will find the solutions to our problems and challenges. I want you to remember this: there is always a way, always a path forward, and always another door waiting to be opened. As it teaches us **James 5:16: "The prayer of a righteous person is powerful and effective."**

It's also important to recognize that, at times, we need the help of professionals. Remember that God has given gifts to many people to help us—including in our mental health. Don't hesitate to go to therapy if you feel it's necessary; it can help you channel your emotions and find the support you need.

That support can also be found in our family, friends, and religious community. I've learned that we need to gather together to worship God. Churches have been organized and created for the benefit of all of us, because within them we find strength, support, and the guidance of leaders and members who can help us during difficult times.

No matter what religion you belong to, worship God according to what you know and in harmony with your faith. Worship Him by attending the church where you congregate and be an active, present member. Doing so will also allow you to be a support to others.

If you don't currently attend a church and would like to learn more about the gospel of Jesus Christ, you can visit this website, where you'll find greater purpose for your life: www. ComeUntoChrist.org.

Can you believe that heaven is closer than we imagine? I do. I feel it every day as I live with my son Moroni. I see it in his smile, in his eyes, and I feel it when he holds my hand, hugs me, and kisses me. In those moments I experience power, tenderness, and above all, a matchless purity that can only come from heaven. I see it in Abby and Mahonri's gentleness. I feel it in the selfless love of my husband as he cares for me.

Heaven touches our lives in many ways: through acts of service, charity, and the genuine love we receive from others. It also manifests in divine interventions from angels, in unexpected miracles, in answered prayers, and in the quiet whispers of the Holy Spirit that guide and comfort us.

Heaven is present in the moments when we feel peace in the middle of the storm, in sincere embraces, in the strength that keeps us moving forward, and in the daily blessings that sometimes go unnoticed. God allows us to see glimpses of His glory here on earth, reminding us that we are never alone and that His love surrounds us constantly.

Going back to our most recent appointment with the cardiologist—and since I wouldn't stop asking questions about Moroni's arteries—the doctor had no choice but to inform me that, yes, the upper artery in his heart is beginning to show signs of a slight narrowing.

The way to detect when an artery is narrowing is by measuring blood flow. In a normal person, this level is 1. A severe level, where intervention would be required, is 3. In his 2024 appointment, Moroni measured at 1.5, and this year, 2025, he measured 1.8. The cardiologist told us we need to continue monitoring him annually.

Maybe our challenges will never end, but we live with happiness, hope, and encouragement. We see the little miracles wherever we go and recognize them every single day—from the moment he wakes up, walks into my room, climbs into my bed, hugs me, kisses me, and smiles.

This past year, our life has changed in ways I can't fully describe. Moroni has progressed more than I ever imagined. His brain now understands many things he couldn't grasp before. Although he still doesn't use words to express himself, if I say something, he tries to repeat it. It's not always clear, but he tries, and that fills me with hope. His teachers have told me that he now counts from one to five in sign language and that he can identify colors—something that once seemed impossible.

Moroni has also made physical progress: he can now eat almost anything, he's begun to jump on trampolines, climb stairs, and even do somersaults.

Just today, I saw him playing with objects and pretending they were food. His brain is beginning to make connections it didn't make before. He lives a happy life—like any other child.

Before, Moroni would only scream out of pain, anxiety, and distress. Today, he still screams loudly, but now it's out of happiness. His screams are expressions of joy, excitement, communication, and playful mischief. Every small milestone is a miracle that reminds me that suffering is not eternal.

I know that one day, my son Moroni's body will be perfect. I know his heart will no longer need surgeries, that his ears will hear clearly, that his feet won't stumble, that his eyes will see perfectly, and that every part of his body will have the strength to do anything.

I know that one day he will speak to me and say, **"Mom, I love you, and thank you for fighting alongside me."** I know his mind will understand how much we love him, and he will value all the love, attention, and sacrifices we have made for him.

That day will come. I don't know when, but I am sure it will.

Thank you, my sweet Moroni, for choosing me to be your mom.

First day of
PRE-K4

My Treasure

Scan the QR Code to follow our journey!

ABOUT THE AUTHOR

My name is Gabby Cornelio. I am a full-time mom, dedicated to the emotional and physical well-being of my children, who face medical challenges and learning difficulties. My role as a mother keeps me constantly on the move—managing therapies, medical appointments, and school accommodations to make sure they receive the support they need. Without any previous experience, I've learned, grown, and discovered new ways to help them overcome their struggles.

That's why I love sharing my life on social media—to offer hope and support to other parents facing similar challenges. Sharing our journey with disability has allowed me to promote inclusion and love. My passion for learning about health led me to discover how important nutrition is to overall well-being. I now enjoy creating healthy recipes—keto, low-carb, and gluten-free—that others can benefit from too.

I'm originally from Mexico, and I moved to the United States at age 21. Learning a new language was challenging, but with perseverance and practice, I began to feel more confident speaking English. I earned an associate degree in Web Design, and I'm currently pursuing a bachelor's degree in Applied Health from Brigham Young University–Idaho to deepen my knowledge in the health field.

I'm passionate about learning and developing new skills. Instead of focusing on one thing, I love challenging myself by exploring various areas and gaining new knowledge. I'm also an artist and illustrator. I brought to life my own children's book inspired by my kids and the importance of communication with nonverbal children. In my free time, I enjoy painting botanical art, creating portraits, and practicing calligraphy.

I love doing things myself—refinishing furniture, transforming spaces, designing and building projects. I always find a way to bring my ideas to life. My creativity knows no limits, and my determination has earned me the nickname "4x4," because I'm truly all-terrain.

I go to the gym every morning with my husband. We love high-intensity workouts—burpees, squats, pull-ups, box jumps, and barbell training. We also cherish weekends at home, which my kids call "movie night," because we love watching movies together as a family.

I am very active in my church, The Church of Jesus Christ of Latter-day Saints. I love serving in callings where I can make a difference. Right now, I work with children, teaching them the gospel through music. I cherish the opportunity to testify of God and Jesus Christ, and my kids love having mom in their class.

I have a deep love for people, which is why I decided to write this book—with the hope of encouraging others to never give up. I'm currently working on several projects, including the release of new books and inspiring stories that will continue to uplift families around the world.

This book is just the beginning...
Want to keep receiving inspiration, resources, and love?

Sign up on my website and download a free companion e-book filled with heartfelt reflections, helpful tools, and uplifting messages for the soul.

You'll also receive positive thoughts, updates on my upcoming book releases, and details about special events coming soon. There's so much more I'd love to share with you! Don't miss out.

Visit: www.gabbycornelio.com
Social Media: @gabbycornelio

OTHER BOOKS BY THE AUTHOR

y Brother Doesn't Speak, But His Heart Does!

My Brother Doesn't Speak, But His Heart Does! is a touching story about the unique bond between Maho and Momo, two brothers who learn to communicate without words. Momo, age four, has a special condition that keeps him from speaking, but through gestures, smiles, and hugs, he expresses more than words ever could.

His older brother, Maho, faces challenges trying to understand him, but with patience and love, he discovers that the heart can communicate better than speech. Together, they show that the love between siblings can overcome any barrier.

More than just a story, My Brother Doesn't Speak, But His Heart Does! is an inspiring guide that reminds us love will always find a way to be heard.

For more information about the author and her work, visit
www.gabbycornelio.com